Alma,

Thank you for engaging every family!

Arne Duncan

101
WAYS TO CREATE

REAL
Family
ENGAGEMENT

Steven M. Constantino, Ed.D.

101 Ways to Create Real Family Engagement

© 2008 ENGAGE! Press
Printed and bound in the United States of America

ENGAGE! Press
411 N. Main Street
Galax, VA 24333

First Printing 2008
ISBN No. 978–0–9814543–1–3
Library of Congress Cataloging–in–Publication Data

CONTENTS

1. Make Sure Your School Says Welcome!
2. Appreciate the Culture of Your Community
3. A Continuous Celebration of Families
4. Directional Signs: Clear, Concise, and Culturally Sensitive
5. Family Parking Only
6. A Culture of Acceptance, Openness, and Value toward All
7. Train Teachers Today for Engaged Families Tomorrow

Domain 2:
Two–Way Communication Between School and Home

Introduction:
We Need Real Family Engagement

Whether you think you can or think you can't,
you're right.

—Henry Ford

Since writing *Engaging All Families* in 2003, I have made thousands of new friends, both in the United States and abroad, as I traveled to hundreds of schools and districts sharing the importance of family engagement. Educators and support staff have embraced the philosophy of engagement: student achievement increases when families are engaged in their children's education. *Engaging All Families* established a framework for engaging families. *101 Ways to Create Real Family Engagement* compliments those principles and suggests ways that a school can further increase student achievement through family involvement.

What is Real Family Engagement?

Real family engagement is data–driven and must translate into increased student achievement. Checking off boxes on a school plan, or submitting one math night as evidence of continuing engagement does not count. The school must nurture relationships with all families and then give them tools to participate in their children's education. These family/school relationships are the foundation for real family engagement.

Igniting a Revolution in Culture

There are no quick fixes in education. New ideas and strategies that benefit children and increase their achievement must be planned, implemented, assessed; and then modified based on those assessments. Unless the school culture changes to embrace the new concepts, reform is not sustainable. Disengaged staff cannot reach disenfranchised families.

Schools and districts have tried many strategies for engaging families. Very few have succeeded in engaging *all* families. Almost none have reached the families who need it most. At best, most have increased the engagement of the already engaged. The chasm between schools and families who are truly in need of support and outreach grows wider as our society changes. Simply put, *strategies alone will not promote real family engagement.*

The first step in building lasting and effective family engagement processes in your school or district starts with one simple word: *relationships.* Without them, there is no engagement.

How This Book is Organized

The book has two parts. Part I shows you how to make cultural changes that support real engagement. Changed values, attitudes, assumptions, and actions, coupled with clear processes, must be in place prior to applying other solutions. This process of changing the culture of your school or district is the first step in increasing achievement through engaged families.

Do not skip Part I. I know you will want to. With precious little time and the need to get right to the "meat" of what this book can offer, you will be tempted to jump to strategies. If you skip Part I, the rest of the book will provide nothing sustainable. Part I gives purpose to the strategies.

Part II of the book focuses on the techniques that will help shape a framework for real family engagement. Included are 101 practical and tested strategies, organized under the four domains of family engagement:

1. Creating a welcoming environment
2. Effective two–way communication
3. Degree of engagement of every family
4. School support for home learning

Each strategy includes a short action plan to start the process. When possible, real–life stories provide a context for ideas presented.

I think you will smile, learn, and be motivated to begin building the relationships that lead to real family engagement. Thank you for the wonderful work you already do on behalf of the school community, and for the benefit of children. Great things can happen when you embrace and create *real* family engagement for every child, every family, every teacher, *every day*.

Steve Constantino
Atlanta, GA

PART 1:

WHAT IS ENGAGEMENT?
WHY DOES IT MATTER?

CHAPTER

ASSEMBLING THE CULTURAL PUZZLE

Schools have a culture that is definitely their own. There are, in the school, complex rituals of personal relationships, a set of folkways, mores, and irrational sanctions, a moral code of conduct.

—Willard Waller, 1932

Cultural Revolution

More than twenty years of research leaves no room for doubt: Family engagement leads to improved student achievement. Increased engagement leads to gains for all students, regardless of socioeconomic status, cultural background, ancestry, or special education status. If we can increase student achievement by increasing engagement, what is keeping us from experiencing the benefits?

At a recent Family Friendly Schools workshop, a school administrator approached me during a break to share a challenge he was facing. A veteran teacher at his school was struggling with classroom control and had repeatedly sent students to the office with disciplinary referrals. After two referrals in a week for one student, the administrator met with the teacher to explore a better solution than more referrals. During this meeting, the following dialogue occurred:

Administrator: "I would like you to contact the parents and try to resolve the situation before referring the student to the office."

Teacher: "I did contact the parents."
Administrator: "When?"
Teacher: "Last semester."

What is the teacher really saying? Do you see family engagement barriers hidden in this exchange?

Barriers to Family Engagement
- *Fear*
- *Isolation*
- *Assumptions*
- *Values*
- *Attitudes*

To create true family engagement, we must examine and remove all of these barriers between the teacher and the families of students.

Eliminate Fear and Build Trust

The issue of trust is foundational to social theory. In *Foundations of Social Theory,* James S. Coleman offers a four–part definition of trust:

1. Placement of trust allows actions that otherwise are not possible (i.e., trust allows actions to be conducted based on incomplete information about the case in hand).
2. If the person in whom trust is placed (trustee) is trustworthy, then the trustor will be better off than if he or she had not trusted. Conversely, if the trustee is not trustworthy, then the trustor will be worse off than if he or she had not trusted.
3. Trust is an action that involves the voluntary placement of resources (physical, financial, intellectual, or temporal) at the disposal of the trustee with no real commitment from the trustee.
4. A time lag exists between the extension of trust and the result of the trusting behavior.

Relationships cannot exist without trust. At the heart of most disengagement is a lack of trust between families and school personnel. Rebuilding and supporting trusting relationships is essential for engaging families in the academic lives of their children. Trust plays a dominant role in eradicating fears that exist in relationships. Fear is one of the most destructive and energy–robbing emotions any of us can experience. Fear can lead to many irrational behaviors and actions.

Countless teachers, administrators, and parents have shared, through our data–collection and research processes, that they fear talking to one another. Teachers fear that calling home to discuss issues with families will bring on a negative confrontation or a long, complicated conversation about the student's issues. Disengaged families may feel intimidated by our language, expertise, and the simple fact that we are "the school." Most damaging is the belief among families that educators simply do not care. Administrators have told us that most parents will do anything to remove blemishes from their child's discipline record or "take up" for their child when there are academic issues. Often these parents are masking their fear with outward anger.

Anger is a Mask for Fear

Fear is deadly in school–family relationships. If we could isolate and eliminate the fear, we could make huge strides in building successful relationships with families.

One superintendent found that parents were dissatisfied with teacher telephone contacts. Teachers did not return parental calls promptly. Other times teachers did not initiate communication when there was a problem. Overwhelmingly, teachers stated that there were not available phones to return or make parental calls. The superintendent had telephones installed in all classrooms. The school district spent a great deal of money on this project.

Two years later, when the district re–surveyed the parents, the displeasure was worse instead of better. The survey ratings had gone down! District administrators were befuddled as to why. At some point, the district asked my opinion of the situation. I felt the issue was not telephone availability, but the teachers' fear of placing the calls. The teachers did not have strategies to be effective communicators, and they did not believe that parental relationships could be improved through phone calls. In essence, the *culture* needed to change.

Employees who fear expressing their views, or who fear retaliation for actions they take, quickly become disengaged. Students who fear teachers or administrators never meet their full potential. Leaders who fear their bosses may squelch innovation. Families who fear retaliation for their opinions and comments often stay silent or communicate in an anonymous way. Where there is not trust or communication, there are no relationships.

In the opening example, the teacher was likely harboring fear about calling the parents. Perhaps there had been a negative encounter earlier when the teacher called. Maybe the teacher had tried to call and received no answer or response. Perhaps the teacher did not think a call would produce a positive result. Whatever the reason, fear at some level played a part in the relational breakdown.

The Preservation Tank

Humans and animals retreat when they perceive hurtful situations. This instinctive self–preservation response is the core issue of isolation in schools and families. When teachers and parents have had negative interactions, they isolate themselves from each other or, to put it another way, build a preservation tank. It is like the old, familiar joke:

Patient: "Doctor, doctor! It hurts when I do this."
Doctor: "Then don't do that."

People do not repeat behaviors that result in negative experiences. Instead, they build a "preservation tank" to insulate themselves from the same experience. The memory of the negative experience, however, lingers.

I was speaking to a group of teachers at their opening–day celebration, and I was sharing this cycle of negative experience, self–preservation, and isolation. I asked the teachers, "Isn't it funny that ten positive things can happen and we forget most or all of them, but one negative event regarding our children, and we remember it forever? These memories, built up over periods of time, cause resentment and frustration on the part of parents. This is the issue we need to understand, be empathetic to, and address with family engagement."

No sooner did the speech end when a woman, whom I learned was an elementary school teacher, made a beeline for me.

"You are so right," she said. "When my daughter was in first grade..." The woman went on to share a negative encounter with a teacher and principal that she felt affected her daughter for the remainder of that school year.

I asked how her daughter was doing now.

"Oh, she's fine. She is married and has a little one of her own."

The degree of detail this woman could recall led me to believe that her daughter was still in elementary school or perhaps middle school, but this woman had nursed these feelings for over twenty–five years! She even admitted that, at times, her experiences tainted her ability and desire to work with parents of her own students.

Let Me Tell You About THAT School

I'm not going to bother to call that school. I am going right to the superintendent.

Do you know what that school did to my son?

Let me tell you why I will not allow my daughter to attend that school.

When parents and families use the expression, "that school," it is an indicator of isolation. If families cannot see themselves as an important component of the school, construction of the preservation tank begins. The perception that educators are unwilling or unmotivated to work with them becomes the reality. This can result from one negative experience or a series of negative experiences. Over time, parents and families alienate themselves from the school and its educational mission. School personnel often misinterpret this isolation as apathy.

When building healthy relationships with parents and families becomes an important component of your effort to help children learn, emptying the preservation tank and increasing connectedness between families and school personnel becomes central to the cultural transformation.

It's Not What You Say; It's What You Do

In this chapter's opening dialogue, it is important to focus on what was *not* said. If we could crawl into the mind of the teacher and find out what assumptions she held, what would we find? *The parents do not care. The parents do not understand. The parents won't act. The parents defend their children.* Understanding the assumptions is crucial if we are to understand why many family–engagement efforts produce less than spectacular results. Assumptions represent a psychological state in which we hold a premise to be true without any factual basis.

As you consider the following statements, think about the underlying assumptions of the speakers:

Statement: "My remedial math class won't do homework, so I just let them do their work in class."
Assumption: *These students are behind because they are not motivated to learn.*

Statement: "I do not allow parents to visit my classroom."
Assumption: *Parents are judging me. Parents are trouble.*

Statement: "As principal, I will decide which parents will be on our school planning team."
Assumption: *I am the professional. I need to control the situation.*

Statement: "If parents would read what we send them, we would not have communication problems."
Assumption: *I have told them everything they need to know. I do not need their input.*

Statement: "Oh, dear. I had that boy's brother. Good luck with him."
Assumption: *He is more of the same. It is either bad genes or bad parents.*

Statement: "If the parents want to talk to me, they will schedule a conference."
Assumption: *It is lack of effort on the parents' part.*

Statement: "If students and parents would just do what they are supposed to do, we would not have half the problems we have."
Assumption: *They are the problem. Be reasonable and do it my way.*

Statement: "The problem is the poor attitudes and behaviors that children come to school with these days."
Assumption: *Poor parenting is the cause. What happened to the good old days?*

The issue is not whether one agrees or disagrees with these statements. The goal is to understand the underlying assumptions. Those listed above are for illustration only. There are many other assumptions that could give rise to those statements. What is important is that assumptions—beliefs for which we have no factual basis—often drive our attitudes and actions. Parents and families are not so naive as to believe us based on what we say. They also watch our actions. *It's not what you say; it's what you do.*

I have attended many back–to–school nights. The principal always gives an opening speech. Without fail, he or she invites the parents to call or visit the school anytime they wish. "Our school," the principal says, "has an open–door policy." The words are clear: *We welcome your participation in your child's education.* However, an open–door policy is only effective if people feel comfortable enough to walk through the open door. The welcoming message must be more than words.

What evidence is there that the "open–door policy" is more than words? Is a telephone and e-mail list printed in the back–to–school program or available to all parents who attend? Is the school's Web site current? Does it allow for direct communication to any staff member, including the principal? Do the teachers reiterate this welcoming message in the classroom? What evidence is there to show the statement is consistent with the way the school operates? What does the school *do* to support what they *say?*

We cannot hide our beliefs and assumptions from others for long. The way we act and interact will eventually reveal the truth. If we really believe that parents and families are full partners in the education of children, our words will be consistent with the evidence and with our actions.

You Could Be Stuck with a Short Cord

Values govern our behavior. Our personal values evolve from external circumstances and can change over time. Values are not something we think about on a daily basis, but they guide our words, thoughts, and actions. Our values dictate who we are as people and members of the community.

Not long ago, a high school invited me to work with their faculty for an afternoon. The staff development coordinator welcomed me when I arrived and tended to my every need. She apologized for one item they could not get for the session: a cordless microphone. I assured her the corded microphone would be just fine and thanked her for her attention to detail, right down to the two bottles of water she provided. She was extremely thoughtful and accommodating.

The room was a large auditorium in a school built in the 1930s. Older school auditoriums often have balconies, reminiscent of old movie theaters. As the teachers trickled in for the session, I noticed they were taking seats in the back row under the protruding balcony. Normally, in situations like this, I make a lighthearted joke to convince people to move a bit closer. Today, however, it was essential. I only had a six–foot microphone cord!

As the teachers filed in, I announced my dilemma and politely asked them to move to the front of the room. Not one person moved. After making the request four times, I gave up and pondered my dilemma. There were thirty rows of empty seats between the teachers and me. They would not come forward and I could not move to them. I decided to work from the front of the room and hope for the best.

Having covered the basics of engagement, and why it is important, I reached the point in the presentation where I address the effect our values have on our ability to engage parents. I used their behavior as the illustration. "When I finish here today, I am going to leave with an impression, right or wrong, positive or negative. When we began today, I told you I had only a six–foot microphone cord. I asked you to move forward to help me interact with you more effectively. Not one of you moved. How am I likely to interpret the value you have placed on this session based on that conduct? You knew my dilemma, yet you chose to spend the afternoon thirty rows away. Why? Is it the topic? Is it the fact that you would rather be somewhere else? Did I forget my deodorant? Think about the message you have sent with your actions.

Your response to the request that you deemed insignificant an hour ago will shape how I perceive *your* engagement and your interest in engaging others."

As you can imagine, the room was silent. More than a few people shifted uncomfortably, trying to decide whether they should move immediately. To their credit, at the first break, many of them did move forward, and we had a great afternoon.

The important message here is that we demonstrate our values and our beliefs in conscious ways—and in ways that we are not conscious of at all. Children quickly discover our values . . . and so do their families.

If you are not on the top of your game as a teacher and you come into school less prepared or motivated than usual, how long does it take your students to recognize that something is different? Every time I ask that question in a workshop, teachers laugh and shout out, "Two seconds" or "Immediately!" Students have the uncanny ability to sense when something is different in us.

If you tell parents that you value their involvement, but you really do not, how long do you think it will take them to figure that out? If we do not value all parents and families, our ability to foster meaningful relationships is nonexistent. As educators, we can see families in one of two ways. We can see them as assets, or we can see them as liabilities. There is no third option.

Not Everyone Can Be Jimmy Buffett

Jimmy Buffett would have us believe that a change in latitude will change our attitude. While I do not discount his idea, most of us cannot change our latitudes fast enough when our attitudes are not where they should be. If we are able to change our assumptions and values about family engagement, however, our attitudes begin to change as well.

Going back to the original discussion at the beginning of this chapter, what attitude do you think the teacher held about the parent, or calling parents in general? I suspect that her attitude was not positive. This is not to say that the teacher should be condemned. We must recognize that most teachers leave their college programs with little or no exposure to working with families, communicating with families, or understanding the academic benefits of family engagement. Many begin their new positions with nothing more than a stack of teacher's manuals and a set of keys. Their experiences shape attitudes about family engagement. The outcome is easy to forecast. Negative experiences usually equal negative attitudes. Poor assumptions lead to poor outcomes.

Conclusion

Shaping school culture to engage all families requires systematic removal of barriers to meaningful participation of families in the academic lives of their children. The daunting nature of changing institutional culture leads many to pursue programs that nibble at the edge of engagement but never address the core issues that could lead to meaningful reform. Real family engagement cannot occur until all members of the school community share the core value of building and sustaining relationships with all families.

CHAPTER

2

CULTURE EATS
CHANGE FOR LUNCH

We are in one of those great historical periods that occurs every 200 or 300 years when people do not understand the world anymore, and the past is not sufficient to explain the future.

—Peter Drucker

Change in organizations is pervasive, especially in education. Consider the most common change initiatives implemented in the last decade: Total Quality Management, Baldrige in Education, Professional Learning Communities, Curriculum Mapping, and so on.

In a study of how education reform has helped or hindered the positive change in schools, Peterson and Deal[1] report the following outcomes:

- Only 2 percent of the schools reported success.
- Forty percent reported the initiatives to be a complete flop.
- Two–thirds of the organizational reform programs studied had stalled, fallen short, or failed.

Organizational culture is often ignored as a performance factor because it refers to the taken–for–granted values, underlying assumptions, and the actions, expectations, collective memories, and definitions present in an organization.[2]

---

1   T. Deal and K. Peterson, *Shaping School Culture: The Heart of Leadership* (San Francisco: Jossey–Bass, 1999).
2   K. S. Cameron and R. E. Quinn, *Diagnosing and Changing Organizational Culture* (Reading: Addison–Wesley, 1999).

You Shape It or It Shapes You

One can spend years reading about and researching the idea of organizational culture as an important conduit to success. Clearly understood are the ideas of values, beliefs, assumptions, and norms, which can alter and change the organization's culture.[3] In the early days of any organization, people set the tone, shape, and direction of the organizational culture. As the organization matures, the culture shapes the people. Only organizations that are willing to open themselves up to a study of their organizational culture and make the modifications necessary to alter that culture will benefit from attempts to create an engaged culture.

The culture of a school dictates the values, beliefs, assumptions, and norms that drive the organization. To gauge your organization's culture, try taking the quiz below.

Family Engagement Culture Quiz

Answer yes or no to the following questions:

_____ Are all families treated with respect by everyone at your school?

_____ Are all families seen as a potential source of valuable expertise?

_____ Do all staff take personal responsibility to engage families?

_____ Do all staff believe that student performance can be improved with family engagement?

_____ Is active family engagement met with enthusiasm by the entire staff?

A school or district may need to re–examine their commitment to family engagement if they cannot answer "yes" to each of the above questions.

---

3   Deal and Peterson, *Shaping School Culture.*

What We Can Do That I Can't Do

A great deal of information on engagement promotes the concept of improved or increased human capital within an organization. Understanding the role of families within the educational parameters of any organization must move beyond the notion of human capital to the idea of social capital.

Social capital refers to those relationships between the school and the families that enhance the development of a child. Unlike physical or human capital, social capital exists in the relationships between persons in the organization. As relationships form and change, so does the capital that the relationships produce. Some argue that the most beneficial, essential, and important component of social capital is trust.

When creating a culture that engages all families, it is essential that the notion of social capital be a central theme in the process. Building human capital does nothing to close the isolation gap that exists between schools and families. Family engagement cannot occur until the organization builds social capital. When the school and families have a mutual respect for one another and depend on one another as partners in education, the result is increased achievement for students.

Initiatives Die, but Cultures Survive

Most change initiatives fail.

Peter Senge

This cornerstone of real family engagement is a belief in the power of families engaged in the learning lives of their children. Often schools look at contextual solutions and find that the outcomes fall far short of expectations. In other situations, schools and districts continue to engage the already engaged, leaving behind those families who could truly benefit from family engagement and partnership. In order for any organization to benefit from family engagement, a belief that family engagement will improve student achievement must be present. Without that belief, a prescriptive process will produce little in the way of additional engagement, lasting change, or achievement for all.

CHAPTER

3

RULES OF
ENGAGEMENT

What is engagement? It might be helpful if we turn to renowned psychologist Mihaly Csikszentmihalyi for a definition. In his
book *Flow*, Csikszentmihalyi defined *flow* as a state or feeling that
people experience when they are performing tasks that completely
engage them, so much so that the participant in the task does not
consciously think about the steps of the task and may very well lose
track of time while performing the task. In his book *Building Engaged
Schools*, Gary Gordon suggests that flow may be the highest form of
engagement

The Gallup Organization is involved in engagement research,
primarily in the private sector. Gallup estimates that low productivity among those workers classified as disengaged costs the American
economy an estimated $300 billion a year.[4] The cost of disengagement
in the educational system is greater than even this astronomical number, as we are preparing the workforce of tomorrow.

Why Wireless Won't Work

> *For a list of all the ways technology has failed to improve
> the quality of life, please press three.*
> — *Alice Kuhn*

Thomas Friedman, author of *The World Is Flat*, focuses our attention on the technological revolution that can connect anyone on the

---

4   G. Gordon, *Building Engaged Schools: Getting the Most out of America's Classrooms* (New York: Gallup Press, 2006).

planet in just a few seconds. After reading his work, I thought, *We may be connected, but we are not engaged.*

Education is still a people–intensive business. Even though it has become more of a commodity of late, engaging people is still a core value that must be present in any school or district that wants to proceed to the next level of success. Technology keeps us connected but does not guarantee engaged relationships.

Daniel Burrus, author of *Technotrends*, suggests that there has never been a revolution in history like the technological revolution that exists today. He indicates that the "status quo has been shattered by technological change."[5] He defines the new status quo as *rapid change.*

Computer technology has transported our society from information to communication. E–mail, instant messaging, uploading, downloading, blogs, chat rooms, and message boards are all normal means of staying connected with one another. Technology has minimized the need for human interaction, which can have adverse effects on the building of social capital and real engagement within organizations.

Much of present–day school reform centers on providing tools and strategies that will allow educators to teach and evaluate student learning effectively. There is an assumption that everyone participating in growth opportunities *wants* to experience self–renewal. This is a false assumption.

If the majority of the people in your organization are at some level of disengagement, it is unlikely that professional development will create improvement. A culture of engagement must include staff, families, and students.

If we want families to become and remain engaged with the educational experiences of their children and support learning outcomes at home, we must ensure the following rules of engagement are intact:

1. Families must find personal meaning and relevance in their children's educational experiences.
2. Families must receive positive interpersonal support from school employees on a regular basis and in a consistent manner.
3. Families must see evidence that their children's school is successful,

5   D. Burrus, *Technotrends: How to Use Technology to Go beyond Your Competition* (New York: HarperCollins, 1993), xii.

safe, and committed to establishing healthy relationships with parents and families.

Negative catalysts provide the stimuli for humans to avoid the catalyst in a self–preserving mode. Understanding this trait puts into perspective the actions of parents and families when faced with something they consider negative, dangerous, or harmful to their children's wellbeing. Consider the following everyday occurrences for parents and families that may be negative catalysts in engaging with their children and their children's school:

- A child comes home crying and not wanting to return to school
- A teacher loses an assignment
- Bullying
- Perceived unfairness in grading
- Perceived unrealistic expectation held by the teacher
- Negative conversation with the teacher or administrator
- Information heard about the school in the community
- Rumors of safety issues at the school

Any one of these simple occurrences can ignite early stages of disengagement.

Living organisms have a built–in desire to preserve themselves and their species. Organisms will seek the elements within their environment that they perceive as beneficial for their survival. The opposite is also true. Living organisms will avoid those elements that reduce their chances for survival or reduce the chances of survival of their offspring. Self–preservation is instinctive. Human beings do not develop in isolation. Isolation, however, is often the first instinctive reaction when faced with a self–preserving set of circumstances.

We Know What Happens to Houses Made of Straw

An organization that does not promote the active engagement of all is like a house made of straw. One good wind, or one powerful wolf, and the house comes tumbling down. If only a handful of people associated with an organization are disengaged, there is the chance that the organization can reverse the disengagement. If the disengagement is widespread, however, the organization as a whole suffers. When a large number of people within the organization are disengaged, we must look to the organization itself for the clues as to why the problem exists.

CHAPTER

THE DOMAINS OF
FAMILY ENGAGEMENT

Family Friendly Schools, LLC promotes the engagement of all families in the academic lives of their children. There are four domains of family engagement that, when positively affected, link family engagement to improved achievement. The four domains are:

1. A welcoming environment for families
2. Effective two–way communication
3. The degree of engagement
4. School support for home learning

A Welcoming Environment

A welcoming environment implies that a school has focused efforts on maintaining an atmosphere that is inviting to families and honors their presence. Care and concern are evident for the comfort of families, especially those intimidated by the school environment. The school culture strongly embraces family engagement. The approachability of administration and staff invites productive relationships with all families. Schools maintain and improve their welcoming and encouraging environment by constantly monitoring, measuring, correcting, and creating higher expectations so that every family member feels welcome, engaged, important, and involved in the school. Training and capacity–building for staff and families will help to ensure continued excellence.

Effective Two–Way Communication

We all recognize that one-way communication is not really communication at all. For a school to effectively reach and engage all families, they must do more than just expand their efforts at improved methods of outgoing communication. They must also strive to develop simple and effective means for families to communicate and respond to administrators and educators at the school.

The organizational culture created at this type of school embraces healthy, two–way communication between the school and all families, regardless of language, time, or other barriers that may exist. The efforts to produce this level of communication are consistent across all types of ethnic and economically diverse families. The school has designed its procedures to include nontraditional families and families who find it difficult to participate in their children's education. Not only are telephones and technology used to communicate, but also home visits and face–to–face communication are common. The school fosters a sense of caring for all families and has numerous mechanisms in place so that families can communicate directly with the staff members who can help them best.

Regular data collection helps the school determine program effectiveness and consider strategies for continued improvement.

Degree of Engagement

The Degree of Engagement primarily identifies, measures, and encourages improvement in the level of commitment a school exhibits towards reaching and engaging all families.

This category suggests a strong commitment on the part of the school to reinforce the family's role in the education of their children. The school must make a significant effort to reach all families, involve all families, and engage all families. Family engagement requires the same continuous–improvement model as other school–improvement goals. The school measures aspects of its ability to reach, connect, and engage all families in the academic lives of children.

Measuring effectiveness not only highlights those areas in need of improvement, but also protects the school from attitudes of complacency with regard to families. Special attention is placed on goals and objectives associated with real family engagement so that all children reach the desired level of academic success. The role of families in the governance of the school is well defined, and processes are in place to allow family input.

School Support for Home Learning

Families need to understand that they have the power to create positive change in their children's learning. They must see themselves as effective partners with the school. They also need to believe that their partnership is critical for increased achievement. In conjunction with this, schools must encourage family efficacy. They can provide the tools for family effectiveness through sharing information and training in learning skills, testing procedures, standards, and other areas of need. Schools can include families in regular staff development opportunities as well, so that in addition to content knowledge, families have a sense of teaching style and strategy.

Creating Real Family Engagement

Listed in Part II are 101 strategies for creating engagement. Categorized by the four domains, all of them have the potential to move your school one step closer to effectively engaging all families. They are not intended to be events or initiatives, nor is it intended that any school would adopt all of them. Creative schools that value the relationship with families have found hundreds of other ways to build effective collaboration with families. Use the ideas in Part II to generate discussion, and unleash the creative and innovative potential in your school to build real family engagement.

PART II:

101 STRATEGIES THAT CREATE REAL FAMILY ENGAGEMENT

DOMAIN

1

CREATING A WELCOMING ENVIRONMENT AT YOUR SCHOOL

1. Make Sure Your School Says Welcome!

We often talk about welcome signs that greet guests coming into the schools. In addition to signs, the appearance of entrances, sidewalks, roadways, and grounds all play a role in creating a welcoming environment for families and students. Guests and students will immediately notice your efforts to "spruce up" around your school. (A welcoming environment has another benefit: Productivity goes up when employees have an aesthetically pleasing workplace.)

Check your outside lighting and your grounds. Adequate lighting for evening activities shows that you are concerned for the safety of all students and families. Trim shrubs to minimize dark areas.

Look at your entrances as a first-time visitor might see them. When you go in and out of a building every day, you do not always notice the peeling paint on the trim, steps, and railings or the scuff marks on the bottom of the doors. Make it a point to repaint these areas every summer. A few gallons of paint can do wonders, but if your budget does not allow for that, seek donations of paint. Invite your local hardware store to collaborate with the school to create a welcoming environment. Be sure to thank them publicly in your school newsletter.

There are two kinds of graffiti. The first kind is vandalism, which defaces the building and is often related to drugs or gang activity. Pledge to have this removed within 24 hours. Quick removal of this graffiti reflects pride in the facility and shows vandals that it will not be tolerated.

The second kind of graffiti is urban art that not only sends a positive message but also shares the artistic abilities of students and promotes pride. You might dedicate one wall or area of your building for a school–commissioned piece of graffiti art. A committee of teachers, parents, and students can select the artwork from student submissions. Set guidelines for appropriateness before the first can of paint is used.

Local nurseries or garden societies will often donate materials or volunteer to assist in school landscaping projects. List your needs in the school newsletter: There may be families with connections to landscaping or gardening businesses. Check the local high school for a horticulture class, a 4–H club, or a similar group. Many of these students will help you with the landscaping in exchange for community service hours. The service hours are a great incentive, but having pizzas delivered might get you even more free labor!

Making the exterior of your building aesthetically pleasing sends a very clear message of value to all guests.

Things to Do:

1. *Work with your school council or school culture teams to create a plan to improve the appearance of the exterior of the school.*
2. *Conduct surveys to get reactions of families and students regarding the new face–lift.*

2. Appreciate the Culture of Your Community

Almost every school in the United States has seen an increase in students for whom English is not their first language. Efforts to meet the needs of non–English or limited–English speaking families are often minimal and center largely on translation of documents and hiring multilingual employees. While these efforts are important, they are not enough to build relationships with families for whom English is not their first language.

Appreciating and celebrating various cultures shows respect and sensitivity for humanity. In addition, when school employees understand the mores and folkways of different cultures, they can better communicate with students and families.

Inviting families to share information about their cultures during staff development programs is a great way to honor the families and provide staff training. Some families may not be comfortable sharing in a large group but might be willing to speak with their children's teachers.

Things to Do:

1. *Offer a cultural celebration, including food, music, art, and clothing. Have a fashion show that highlights native clothing. Display the national flags and post interesting facts about the flag and the country.*
2. *Highlight a different culture each week or month. Identify families that can assist with learning units in classes and encourage them to do so. Create cross-curricular projects that have culture and ethnicity as a focus.*
3. *Help teachers and staff appreciate different cultures by taking them on a bus tour of neighborhoods. Have individual family members on hand to greet the bus, welcome the staff, and share information about their culture and neighborhood.*
4. *Develop a plan that promotes the celebration of culture throughout the school year.*

3. A Continuous Celebration of Families

An effective means of building family relationships is to celebrate them. In classrooms or at grade levels, highlighting families makes an important social and psychological connection for the student between home and school life.

Give students a disposable camera to take pictures of their families. They can share their families' heritage and ethnicity by writing stories or listing their favorite activities, foods, and traditions. The pictures and stories can be mounted and displayed during the week or month. Invite family members to visit the school and talk to the class about their jobs, their home country, and other areas of interest. Honoring families for their service to the armed forces or community is also another way to promote the concept of family celebration.

At the secondary level, students can use photos in an autobiography assignment that includes their family members. Display the pictures at open houses or special events to celebrate families. Establish a rotating student/family hall of fame.

Things to Do:

1. *Create a program to celebrate families on a continuous basis.*
2. *Designate an existing bulletin board or hallway as a family celebration area.*
3. *Purchase digital or disposable cameras for family pictures.*
4. *Help teachers create lessons that celebrate and acknowledge all families.*

4. Directional Signs: Clear, Concise, and Culturally Sensitive

At South Cobb High School in Austell, Georgia, principal Grant Rivera evaluated the ease of finding the school entrances from the parking lot. Dr. Rivera discovered that guests unfamiliar with the school would have difficulty finding their way around the multi–building facility. There were the main school, the fine arts center, and the magnet center, none of which were clearly identifiable or marked for visitors. Dr. Rivera enlisted the help of his staff and the community to install informational and directional signs. Guests on the campus frequently voiced their appreciation of the signs.

Schools can be complex mazes to many families. The more effort put into helping people navigate around and through the school, the more likely that parents will make repeat visits. Families feel welcome and comfortable in a school that includes directional signs and written information in their primary language.

Things to Do:

1. *Pretend you are new to your school and are standing on the edge of the property. Can you find the parking lot? Are you able to find the places you want to go from the parking lot? If not, create signs and directions that make navigating your school easy for all.*
2. *Again, travel to the edge of your school property. Follow the instructions in the suggestion above but, this time, pretend you do not read or speak English.*
3. *Work with community groups, local businesses, parent groups, and staff to secure the signs necessary to make navigating your school and grounds easy for all.*
4. *In addition to language, assess the degree to which directions are clear for guests and families who are blind or visually impaired.*

5. Family Parking Only

I always discuss the "visitors" vs. "guests" idea in workshops. Simply put, there is a reason that Wal–Mart has a greeter and Disney calls its visitors "guests." They want to make people feel welcomed and appreciated.

Designated parking is good customer service and sends a clear message that thought and care regarding the busy and complicated lives of parents and families is foremost in the mind of the school. Go beyond "guest" parking and create some "family" parking areas. Some schools have taken this suggestion and created special parking signs that have the name of the school plus the words *family parking* clearly visible for all to see. Most schools designate parking for the administration, staff, students, and visitors. I have seen special places for secretaries and cafeteria workers as well. However, rarely do I see a sign that says "family parking." What a tremendous impression you could make on family guests if you replaced the "principal parking only" sign with "family parking." I am quite sure it would create a buzz in your community.

Things to Do:

1. *Designate ten parking spaces for families at your school by creating signs that say "(Name of School) Family Parking."*

6. A Culture of Acceptance, Openness, and Value toward All

It is easy for educators to become cynical and distrustful when many of our dealings with families seem to be negative. When a parent arrives at school unannounced, we quickly assume there is a problem. Distraught or upset parents may believe that they will only be heard when they become belligerent. I believe there is a lot of evidence to support these feelings. However, the reverse can also be true. Consider the story below about Dr. Grant Rivera, his family friendly ideals, open mind, and positive attitude about all families.

Dr. Rivera became principal of South Cobb High School in July 2005, just one month before the school year began. He brought a family friendly mentality to South Cobb, which had a history of declining test scores and low community morale. Let's look at some of the things he did to give parents a voice.

In his daily interactions with families, Dr. Rivera made time to speak with all who wished to see him—whether they had an appointment or not. He worked closely with the office staff to provide good customer service and reminded them that an unhappy customer could become a satisfied customer in about two minutes. He advocated for parents to visit classrooms while classes were in session and welcomed parents to the school at any time. Though his faculty and staff were skeptical at first, they quickly discovered that this philosophy paid big dividends. Dr. Rivera was unyielding in his determination to apply principles of fairness, open mindfulness, and a positive attitude.

On November 7, 2005, just four months after Dr. Rivera became principal, the following letter appeared in the mail. The author had a reputation as a "difficult parent."

> *Dear Dr. Rivera,*
>
> *I wanted to send you a letter regarding the new direction that South Cobb High School has taken during this school year. I was very excited to see a new principal arrive after the experiences I had last year when I wanted to observe my son's classroom. He is an essentially good kid who sometimes needs a push to get his attention focused on what he needs to be doing. After watching our son's grades fall, my husband and I decided that I would attend a day of school with him. I had done this one other time when*

he was in seventh grade, and it seemed to grab his attention and get him refocused on his schoolwork. I entered the school, sent my son on to his class, and went to the office to register as a visitor. I had my ID and asked where to sign in to attend classes with my son. The office staff acted like this had never been done before. I was asked to wait to see the principal to get permission to attend classes with my son. The principal stated that I could not go to classes. After much debate and my declaration that if I could not go to classes, I would be withdrawing my son from this school, I was allowed to attend, but only after a letter was sent to each classroom teacher and they individually approved my visit. This interaction gave the impression that the school had something to hide.

When I received an e–mail from one of my son's teachers about his grades in October of this year, I again decided to attend school with him for the day. I came hoping that the "family friendly school" was more than just a saying. The office staff greeted me and introduced me to the grade level administrator. The administrator was very friendly and was happy to see a parent involved at this stage of a child's school career. She assisted me in finding the teacher's room and told me I was welcome anytime. My day was well spent. All my son's teachers welcomed me, and I was very impressed with the material covered and the way it was covered.

I have also been impressed with the whole atmosphere of the school. This school needs a strong involved principal and I can see this every time I attend a football game. Last Friday at the game, we were sitting near the band section. I was so impressed that you came over to speak with the band regarding their show of spirit for the football team; but then, you proceeded to tell them about the girl's softball team victories. You told them about the fan bus that you were getting together, so that they could ride for free to attend the game and show support for the girl's softball team. I could see a genuine care and concern in the way that you interacted with these students. It is a great thing to witness good people in action in education.

I would like to thank you and your staff for all you do and hope that you will be at South Cobb High School for years to come. I believe that you and your staff can make a great impact on students in the South Cobb community.

Sincerely,
(Parent Name)

Things to Do:

1. *Promote a culture of acceptance, communication, and value toward all families.*
2. *Do not judge families on previous behaviors. Work to change your culture and receive a letter like the one Dr. Rivera received.*
3. *Identify disgruntled parents and turn them into fans and supporters of the school.*

7. Train Teachers Today for Engaged Families Tomorrow

Provide all employees with family engagement training through workshops that share research findings and the practical applications of that research. Have a plan to provide training for new staff members who were not included in your initial staff development. It is important not to shelve family engagement to make way for another initiative. Family engagement should be ongoing and infused into the ideas, planning, and execution of all strategies for school improvement.

Remember to include support staff in your family engagement training. Secretaries, assistants, and paraprofessionals are often the first point of contact with families. Cafeteria workers, custodians, clinic staff, and transportation employees also have contact with parents. Their ability to communicate, share accurate information, and provide excellent service will make the difference between a great family engagement program and a mediocre one.

Family engagement is not an initiative that adds responsibilities to already overburdened teachers and staff. Rather, it builds on the positive things they are already doing and opens doors so that families can be true partners in education.

Things to Do:

1. *Include professional and support employees in staff development, stressing the benefits of family engagement.*
2. *Provide staff with a forum for sharing and learning new strategies that support family engagement.*
3. *Train support staff to provide outstanding customer service to students and families.*
4. *Have a plan to train new staff members who missed the initial seminars and consider assigning mentors to help with the family engagement concepts employed at your school.*

8. Fabulous Family Feedback

No matter where I travel, I have the opportunity to rate the service provided to me. I can rate my satisfaction with my stay at a hotel, a meal in a restaurant, my airline experience, my rental car experience, and even a cab ride. Businesses understand that customer satisfaction is the lifeline to success.

Consider a recent experience I had with my wife's car. I needed a tire replaced and the remaining tires rotated. I contacted the service department where we bought the car and spoke to a customer service representative. This representative explained to me that he would oversee my service and work for my satisfaction. He then offered me an appointment to come in that very day and noted that the waiting area had refreshments, satellite television, and free wireless Internet access.

I arrived forty–five minutes early and told the receptionist that I was early and certainly understood waiting. Within two minutes, my customer service agent came to the foyer and introduced himself to me. He explained how long the service would take and moved it up on the schedule since I was early.

Because I had not been to this repair facility before, the agent escorted me to the waiting area. Then, he asked if he could do anything to make my wait more pleasant. About half–way through the one hour time I was quoted, my agent came out to the waiting area to inform me that the repairs were right on schedule. Twenty minutes later, he returned to inform me that the tire service was finished and they were washing my car.

At this time, he told me that I would receive a follow–up phone call to rate my experience at the service center. He said, "Mr. Constantino, we strive on getting a rating of five (the highest), and if our service center or I have not provided you with service that allows us to get that rating, I would like you to help me improve." He gave me his business card and a copy of the service–rating questions that I would be asked. When the phone call came, I rated my experience a five . . . because it was!

Daily, parents and family members come to the school to get information, resolve issues, or drop off forgotten lunches, homework, uniforms, and projects. These guests leave with an impression about the school, but we rarely ask them for feedback on their experiences.

Are the guests in your building having positive interactions with your staff? If you do not know the answer to this question, then the time has come to do something about it.

Upon entering a school, parents and families usually have to sign in. When they do, give them a service response card with questions like those below, to be rated on a one–to–five scale, with five being the most positive:

- Did you find what you were looking for?
- Were you treated respectfully?
- Did our staff help you?
- Did you get the information you sought or solve the problem you hoped to solve?
- Please feel free to write comments on the back of this card.

Invite them to fill out the card before they leave and drop it in one of the boxes located around the school. This type of feedback is critical in creating welcoming school environments and building a positive culture among parents, families, staff, and students.

Things to Do:

1. *Develop your own service response card, customizing it to your school's needs. Be sure that cards are in the native language of the guest.*
2. *Monthly, record the responses and provide staff with ratings of guest experiences. Work to improve ratings or maintain them if they are already high.*
3. *Encourage good service with incentives that will motivate staff to provide excellent customer service.*
4. *Develop a "strive for a five" (the highest rating) mentality among all school staff.*

9. A Simple Bookmark for All Guests

Student safety and building security are top priorities in schools today. The danger in our society, coupled with high–profile episodes of school violence, gives all educators pause to rethink school access to anyone beyond students and faculty. This has caused a significant problem for schools promoting an open–door philosophy of a family friendly school.

Remind families throughout the school year *why* security processes are in place. Explain the locked gate and the sign–in process so that parents expect and cooperate with the procedures. One middle school handled this situation as part of their welcome sign:

Welcome!
We Care About the Safety of Our Students and
We Care About You!
Please Sign In!
Thank You! We Appreciate You!

Most schools want parents and guests to sign–in and obtain a guest badge. (Notice that I did not say visitor badge.) In addition to providing a guest badge, consider handing every guest a small bookmark. Print school contact information on one side of the bookmark. The other side can include information that is important for parents and families to know and can change periodically. For example, as the testing period approaches, the bookmark might have a copy of the testing schedule, a reminder of the importance of attendance on test days, and suggestions for a good breakfast for their child.

A bookmark is a quick, inexpensive way to share relevant and important information with parents. You can change bookmarks by the month or the event, depending on what you feel is important to share. Keep previous bookmarks on hand. When parents say they received one earlier, show them all the different bookmarks available, and make sure they have received one of each. This a great way to share information and it allows for friendly communication during the sign–in procedure. You can purchase perforated bookmark sheets at an office supply store or print bookmarks on tag–board and cut with the paper cutter.

Do not limit your creativity to bookmarks. You might consider cards, tear–offs, and other items that will grab the attention of visitors and communicate important information.

Things to Do:

1. *Create bookmarks or other informational items to give to those who sign in for your building.*
2. *In your next survey, ask parents and families how they get information about the school. List the various methods you have used to disseminate information, including your newsletters, bookmarks, phone communications, and school marquees. Use their responses to determine the effectiveness of the different methods of communication.*

10. Make Back–to–School . . . Back to School!

Most districts schedule Back–to–School or Open House celebrations weeks after the beginning of the school year. This scheduling
allows just enough time for attitudes to set in, problems to appear, and
a poor grade or two to surface. By the time schools celebrate this traditional event, the opportunities to create strong, trusting, and meaningful relationships with families are already gone.

Consider moving the back–to–school celebration to the opening hours of the school year. Visit local employers and seek flextime
for family members to spend a few hours at school on opening day.
Be sure to invite the employers to attend, too. Many fire departments
raise funds with pancake breakfasts. Ask whether they would hold one
at school on opening day. Do not worry about passing out syllabi and
other information. Use this time to build relationships and to celebrate
with the students, families, school staff, and community leaders. As
this celebration becomes an annual event, more and more parents will
attend and more and more businesses will support your efforts.

Another suggestion is to celebrate the new school year before
it even starts. David LaRose, Assistant Superintendent for School
Support in the South Kitsap School District, shares how his school
district gets the year off to a remarkable start.

The South Kitsap School District is located in Port Orchard,
Washington. In March 2003, the school board approved a strategic
plan that included effective parent and community involvement as
one of its main pillars for student success. To introduce the "Family
Friendly Schools" concept, the district contracted with Family Friendly
Schools, LLC to conduct a seminar for teams comprised of staff and
parents from each school and department in the district. One of the
shared outcomes was the creation of "Welcome Back" celebrations at
each school. These varied from a "meet your teacher ice cream social"
to a full–scale barbecue for all families. In addition to school celebrations, the South Kitsap "Family Friendly District" team developed a
"Back to School Celebration" for all district families. The goal of the
inaugural event was to get students and families excited about going
back to school, to get information out to the families, and connect
families with resources in the community—doing it all in a fun, positive atmosphere. Held around the high–school track in mid–August
from eleven in the morning until two in the afternoon, the event fea-

tured a children's performer, hands–on activities, crafts, and school bus rides. Organizations and businesses who focus on children and their families like the Boy Scouts and Girl Scouts, the Health Department, local karate dojos, and dance studios hosted informational booths around the track.

To promote the celebration, the school mailed postcards to all families. They displayed banners in town, on top of the school, and on the side of a school bus parked in high–traffic areas. Three hundred people attended, most of them "hard–to–reach" families who were drawn to this free event. Exit surveys reflected a high degree of approval, with the only negative comment being that no food was available, although bottled water, popsicles, and popcorn were provided at no cost.

Following the success of the first "Back to School Celebration," the South Kitsap Family Friendly District team committed to holding this event annually. In the second year, the event drew more than five hundred people!

The Family Friendly District team enlisted the help of community organizations, including Foursquare Heritage Church, whose pastor was very active in the community. The church furnished free school supplies, staffed additional games, and provided inflatable "bouncy" toys. Advertisement, promotion, and activities for the second event were essentially the same as the first, with the addition of participation in a summer parade: All attendees carried balloons and marched behind the high school band and cheerleaders.

Student leadership organizations and clubs also assisted with the event. To address the "lack of available food" response on the survey from the first event, a booster club provided free hot dogs and chips. With a donation jar, they were able to cover costs and even realize a profit.

When asked to analyze their success, the South Kitsap School District came up with these suggestions:

- Have the event the same weekend every year. Keep it short and high energy (three hours is perfect).
- Select event chairpersons who are dedicated to the family friendly ideals. Be sure they have collaborative leadership styles and work well together. (SKSD had three co–chairs.)
- Choose committee chairpersons to oversee different segments

of the event, such as entertainment, vendors, donations, logistics, volunteers, arts, crafts, and games.

- Enlist the community. Involve business leaders, church leaders, and parents in the planning stages. Seek major sponsorship from at least one organization.
- Have each school in the district represented at the event. Parent organizations and staff members can actively promote their schools while sharing contact information, grade–level supply lists, and registration procedures and requirements.
- Communicate, communicate, communicate. The postcards mailed in mid–summer went to every family and allowed them to plan for the event. The banners served as a visual reminder as the date approached and reached community members who were not on the mailing lists.
- Invite family– and child–oriented organizations and businesses to have informational booths at the event. These organizations might include dance and karate groups, storytellers, arts councils, local education foundations, and recreation or sports clubs.
- Create a festival experience with balloons, free food, music, games, and prizes for all!
- Pamper your vendors: Bring them water, sunscreen, and a smile.
- Encourage non–exhibiting merchants to donate water, popsicles, prizes for raffles, school supplies, or anything kid–related.
- Bring social service groups to the event. United Way, health departments, police, and others can provide helpful information and resources for families. Ask the local fire and rescue departments to provide a first–aid station as well as share information about their services.
- Give school bus rides. This is a huge hit with younger attendees.
- Include activities and music for all grade levels.
- Make most events and items free. (*Free* is a draw and communicates that you *invest* in your families.)
- End the event with a parade! Attendees join the marching band and cheerleaders in this grand finale parade.
- Provide an exit survey (and pencils) for everyone. This is an invaluable tool to improve the celebration for the next year!
- Last, remember to have fun. Attitudes are contagious.

Not only does this event start the year on a fun and enthusiastic note, it also initiates and enhances trusting, caring relationships with the children and families served by the South Kitsap School District.

Things to Do:

1. *Eliminate the traditional back–to–school night. In its place, initiate the Family Celebration Day during the first day of school. Alternatively, consider the South Kitsap model and design a celebration to be held before the start of the school year.*
2. *Help parents and families get a few hours off work to attend the event. This can only be accomplished by working with community and business leadership.*
3. *Encourage hospitals, churches, social services, the fire and police departments, and other community agencies to be on hand and lend their special talents, such as operating a first aid station.*
4. *Let the teachers know that it is a time to meet and greet, to establish trust and build relationships.*
5. *Make all phone numbers, Web site URLs, and e–mail addresses available for everyone who attends. Consider making refrigerator magnets with this information on them.*

11. "Out Standing" Staff

No, that is not a typographical error. One important way for school administrators and staff to show their commitment to the safety of the students is to be visible—that is, out standing in the bus zone and student drop–off zones during arrival and dismissal times. An administrator at the front door can greet families and students entering the building. An administrator in the parking lot has the opportunity to open car doors, greet the students, and speak or wave to every parent dropping off students. This face–to–face interaction is invaluable for building relationships.

From a school perspective, the principal begins to associate the family members with the students. It is priceless when the principal recognizes a family member at an athletic event, in the grocery store, or at a community event and asks, "How is (student name) doing?" Personal interaction builds trusting relationships.

When principals and assistant principals are visible, families do notice. Families appreciate that the principal values their children enough to meet and greet them each morning.

Similarly, at the close of a school day, place staff members in locations where they have opportunities to interact with families. At a high school, the principal may purposely walk the "pick–up" line of cars or go into the student parking lot where students and families congregate. Whether your schedule permits morning, afternoon, or both, the idea is simple: Staff members (principals included) need to be in strategic locations. Their time and visibility create significant dividends in welcoming guests on the school campus.

Things to Do:

1. *Target campus locations where families and students gather on a regular basis.*
2. *Designate staff members to be at such locations each day to greet each student and family, and provide general supervision.*
3. *Wave and smile at every student and adult who passes!*
4. *Principals, given the demands on your time, it is easy to let these opportunities for visibility slip away. Make a commitment to be available and visible during these peak times.*

12. You've Got Company

If you have invited a guest to your home for dinner, you would be sure that everything was in its proper place. You would wash the dirty dishes, neatly fold the newspapers that were scattered on the floor, and put away any clutter. Your efforts make your dinner guests feel comfortable and welcome in your home.

The same is true for your school. First impressions of guests influence their generalizations about campus safety, security, and cleanliness. The administrative team and custodial staff need to ensure that the front of the campus is clean and presentable. As parents bring their students to school, as students disembark from buses, and as neighbors drive by, they make judgments about the facility. Your attention to detail will increase the likelihood of positive impressions.

Preparing for school guests may be as simple as a daily walk along the front of the school, picking up litter and checking for any safety hazards. For schools with financial resources or business partners, consider landscaping around the entrances with a colorful burst of seasonal flowers.

Things to Do:

1. *Assign a staff member to check main entrances each morning and afternoon before arrival and dismissal times.*
2. *Ask the following questions:*
   a. *Are the grounds near the front entrance litter-free?*
   b. *Are driveways used by parents and buses clear?*
   c. *Are the major road and sidewalk areas near the front of the school clear of trash?*

13. A Family Friendly Focus

Just as we would share school improvement goals with our school community, the same should be true regarding our goals for family engagement. Be sure your community understands your vision for a family friendly school.

Opportunities for promotion of school priorities are as varied as the students and families we serve. Consider the following avenues to promote your school's priorities:

- School letterhead
- "Signature" line to be included at the bottom of all internal and external e-mails
- Welcome message on school phone
- Web site

The message is as important as the medium. School leadership should determine, *honestly* and *accurately*, where your school is on the continuum of real family engagement. Align school goals and external communication accordingly. Expect to be accountable for beliefs and actions or lack thereof.

Disengaged families may be slow to recognize changes in school matters, such as curriculum, instructional strategies, and student achievement. However, families can determine the degree to which they feel valued and respected through their school–home interactions. Tailor your message according to your ability to "walk the walk." Consider the following proclamations based on your progress along the Family Friendly Schools continuum:

- Smith Middle School—Striving to be a Family Friendly School
- Jones High School—A Family Friendly School
- Hill Elementary School—Every Child, Every Teacher, Every Family, Every Day
- Can you think of other ways to incorporate a family friendly message?

Take every opportunity to let everyone know that you are family friendly!

Things to Do:

1. *Determine, through the domains presented in this book, how you can strive to be a family friendly school.*
2. *Take every opportunity (voice, written, electronic) to promote your Family Friendly vision.*
3. *Unite your school behind the common purpose of becoming family friendly!*

14. The Family Friendly Front Office

As a guest, would you feel welcome in the front office of your school? Choose one from the following that best describes the climate of your front office or lobby:

A. Stock trading floor on Wall Street
B. Doctor's office
C. Department of Motor Vehicles
D. A school that is family friendly

Whether the final destination is a classroom, cafeteria, or administrative office, most schools have a central location for guests to check–in. This "first stop" makes a "first impression." Be sure staff and environment reinforce the welcoming message of a family friendly school.

Consider your experience in doctors' offices, schools, and businesses. Do you feel welcome? Are your questions or concerns addressed in a manner that shows you are valued? Does the office have a friendly or sterile feel?

Every person who comes into the school leaves with an impression, including delivery persons as well as members of the school family. Adults (like children) will feel more welcome when they find a caring staff and inviting environment. Consider the following variables that send a welcome message to all who enter the "first stop" of their journey through your school:

1. Have a receptionist, secretary, or student aide welcome each person entering the office.
2. Post student pictures, artwork, and success stories in a tasteful and appropriate manner.
3. Have a bilingual staff member available to facilitate communication with non–English speakers.
4. Place a "Book of Success"—a binder of student pictures and news articles about the school—where guests can read it while waiting.
5. Provide appropriate seating and lighting.
6. Make brochures, pamphlets, and other items available for the taking.

7. Many retail businesses and restaurants use professional "shoppers" to evaluate services. Schools can do the very same. Have someone unknown to the school staff enter the front office and make a reasonable request that gives this person an opportunity to sit for ten to fifteen minutes in the office. Ask this person to make notes regarding atmosphere, customer service, and the degree to which he or she and other guests who enter the office were welcomed.

Things to Do:

1. *Review the attributes of a friendly office. Compare your office to the standards presented.*
2. *Be committed to serving all families who enter your office.*

15. Marquee Messages: Information Only or Call-to-Action?

Regardless of whether you have a traditional plastic–letter sign or a modern electronic visual display, a school marquee is a visible communication medium for the community. Think about the messages you have seen on school marquees. How many are exclusively information–based? Typically, you will see dates of meetings, school holidays, sports events, or meetings.

Now, consider the ad billboards on the highway or ads on television and radio. Advertisers pay large amounts of money for these ads. They don't want to give you only information; they want to entice you to take action.

Even in the limited space of a school marquee, you can apply this advertising concept and move from an "information–only" message to a "call–to–action." Your message can inform, invite, and engage anyone who drives past the school. The following are examples of how to trigger greater reflection (and action!) among students and families:

1. Report Cards Mailed Home on Dec. 15 – Parents, Are You Engaged in Your Child's Success?
2. Student Holiday April 2–6 – Our Staff Wishes Your Family a Safe and Enjoyable Holiday. Success Starts Again April 9 – Be Prepared.
3. Community Forum Sept. 19 – State of the School Address – We Look Forward to Seeing You!

Connecting the marquee to learning is also beneficial in promoting family engagement. Posting the SAT "word of the day" or the character education "word of the week" is an easy and cost effective way to promote engaging all families . . . every day!

Things to Do:

1. *Determine which messages and announcements are most important – prioritize. Not every athletic event or meeting needs to be posted on the school marquee. If you had five seconds (considering traffic flow), what message would you share with a member of your school community?*
2. *Establish a calendar for the school semester or year; determine what*

messages will be posted and for what amount of time.
3. *Transform "information–only" announcements to a "call–to–action."*
4. *Use your marquee to connect the public to learning.*

16. Replicate the Wal–Mart Way

In 1969, Sam Walton, founder of Wal–Mart, set out to create an improved shopping experience for America. Today, Wal–Mart is perhaps the single most successful retail business in the world. An important component to that success was Walton's belief that valuing people is the key to creating a successful business. With this in mind, Sam Walton created the "Wal–Mart Greeter." Comments like "Welcome to Wal–Mart, how are you today?" and "Thanks for coming today!" have become staples of the Wal–Mart experience.

You can replicate the Wal–Mart idea with a greeter to welcome students and guests to your school. Enlist the help of community volunteers—parents, senior citizens, or members of local clubs and organizations—who are willing to give their time as school greeters.

Create a button, vest, or name tag that identifies them as greeters. Think about the Wal–Mart greeter's vest. Printed on the vest is the question, "May I help you?" Take this very simple idea and make it work for you. If you can't afford a vest, create a name tag or a button that says, "I am here to help."

Things to Do:

1. *Work with parents, senior citizens groups, clubs, and organizations within your community to build a network of people willing to volunteer to be a greeter at your school.*

2. *Invest time teaching and providing your new greeters information about your school. Supply them with answers to frequently asked questions, familiarize them with the building, and provide them with maps and other materials to help them be effective.*

3. *Remind all greeters to smile and be enthusiastic about welcoming parents and families to your school.*

4. *If your school serves a multi–lingual community, use greeters who are fluent in different languages. Advertise to the community when they will be available to assist families.*

17. Put a Face with a Map

Many schools provide a map of the building to assist guests. The following map idea will also help guests learn the names of many staff members.

Take digital photos of personnel. Include these pictures, with each person's name and position, on the map. If the school is too large to place all staff on the map, concentrate on those key personnel that families need to know. This list might include the office staff, cafeteria staff, librarians, counselors, and parent resource staff. Many schools who have adopted this idea report that parents and families appreciate knowing what the person whom they are trying to find looks like. It is a simple idea but one that reaps big dividends.

Things to Do:

1. *Take digital photos of school personnel.*
2. *Create maps of the school with photos embedded.*
3. *Ask greeters to point out staff members and building locations when they distribute maps to guests.*

18. "You Get One Chance to Make a Good First Impression"

In our Family Friendly Schools workshops, I have participants go through an exercise called "Be Our Guest." We ask each table of participants to brainstorm a list of things that they would do in their own home to prepare for a guest. The lists are always long, and we have some fun talking about things like dogs, cat litter, and messy spouses! Each group then looks at its list and checks those items that are appropriate to do in preparing for guests at a school function. It is quite amazing that a large number of the items transfer to the second list. Within a few minutes, each team has a "to do" list for making a positive impression on visiting families.

I am sure your family, like mine, told you that you get one chance to make a first impression. The same philosophy holds true for your school. Families want to know their children attend a school that is clean, safe, drug–free, and conducive to learning.

Your custodial staff probably does an outstanding job making sure the school is cleaned and ready to go each morning. Consider though, that most families do not see the school in the morning. The majority of families see the school during events, meetings, concerts, and workshops that take place in the evening—after a long day of students and staff working in the building. Let's face it, after dismissal each day, the school building is not at its best!

Most custodial staffs have a routine to clean the building each night. For example, at Stonewall Jackson, each member of the custodial staff cleaned a specific section. The bulk of the work started on the third floor and worked its way down to the first floor. Unfortunately, most public events were held on the first floor. What is the solution? Change the cleaning routine.

Work with your custodial staff and keep them informed of evening events. Have them change their routine on evenings when meetings and events are taking place. For example, if there is a concert in the auditorium, ensure that the outside area near the entrance has been picked up, the doors are wiped of student fingerprints, the floors are mopped in the lobby, and the bathrooms closest to the auditorium are cleaned. By cleaning these areas first, guests get a wonderful impression of the school.

If your school is used for community events, have the custodial staff clean the public areas first. Always put your best foot forward when company is coming!

Things to Do:

1. *Share and review the evening calendar of events with your custodial staff.*
2. *Create a plan to clean indoor and outdoor public areas first on those evening when events are taking place.*
3. *Remember to thank and praise the custodial staff for a job well done.*

19. You Are Here!

Shopping malls have "You Are Here" signs located near each entrance. The signs include a detailed map with a color–coded directory of every store located in the mall. To help you find your way to the desired destination, there is a well–marked "X" on the map that indicates, "You are here."

You can use this mall concept to help guests find their way around your school. Dr. Ed Wong, former principal at Ensign Middle School in Newport Beach, California, created numerous "You Are Here" signs for guests to navigate the complicated, multi–building campus.

Things to Do:

1. *Work with teachers and parents to determine locations for "You Are Here" signs.*
2. *Work with local retailers, Chamber of Commerce, business partnerships, and other community agencies to provide sources of revenue to get the job done.*
3. *Ensure that your sign shows directions to frequently visited locations, such as the main office, satellite offices, the guidance office, the gymnasium, the cafeteria, the auditorium, and the nurse's office.*
4. *Display your school name and mascot clearly on the sign. If space permits, post your school slogan or a fragment of your mission statement that best communicates your desire to help all children learn.*

20. A Follow Up to a Visit

How many families enter your school each day? Do you keep a record? Most of the time the answers are "I do not really know" or "No." Many schools ask that parents to sign in when visiting. Schools often ask parents to sign their children out if they are picking them up before dismissal time. Schools can have sign–in sheets for appointments, meetings, or other activities that may be happening. In many schools, security plans require all guests to sign in. Here is a neat idea for the sign–in sheets that will generate big dividends.

At the end of each day, review the sign–in sheets and choose two names. Take a minute to call and ask them about their experience while visiting the building. Were they treated courteously? Did they have any problems with parking or locked doors? Did they know where to go? If they needed help, did someone help them?

At first, families might think it odd to receive a phone call about their experiences dropping off their child's lunch! But do not worry; the call leaves a huge *"we care"* message in the mind of the family. The visitor will likely mention to others that someone took the time to call and ask. One three–minute phone call pays huge dividends when establishing a warm and welcoming environment for the school.

The additional benefit is the immediacy with which a parent or family member can communicate a problem or negative experience. Listening to concerns and pledging to resolve the issue before the next visit assures the parents and families that we care. Remember to develop that "strive for a five" mentality!

Things to Do:

1. *Determine how many "sign–in" or "sign–out" documents there are in your building. Check the main offices, nurses' office, and student counseling office. You might be surprised at the guest records they have available.*

2. *Look at the notes that parents and families write for early releases. This is another area of data that helps you understand who is coming and going in your building throughout the day.*

3. *Pick two or three guests to call each day. Ask them about their experiences during their visit. Thank them for their support and invite them back.*

21. A Positive Sign!

Take an inventory of the informational signs that help families and students in your school. We often use "negative" signs in schools, such as "No parking," "No Entry," or "Off Limits." Whenever possible, turn your negative signs into positive signs.

For example, many schools have a sign that says "Faculty Parking Only." If you are a guest, you are confronted with a somewhat negative sign and no knowledge of where to park. Remedy this by directing your guests to where they may find parking. For example: "This area is for faculty parking. Family/Guest parking is located behind the gym."

The same holds true for entrances. Instead of, "No Entry," consider, "Welcome, our Guest Entrance is located near the flag pole." Turn any negative messages into positives ones by simply rewording them.

Things to Do:

1. *Take inventory of your "negative" and "positive" signs.*
2. *Work to create positive message signs that direct, encourage, and support all parents, families, and guests.*
3. *Set a goal of replacing all of the negative signs with positive ones!*

22. Kiss and Learn

Just about every airport, bus station, and train station has an area for drivers to drop off passengers at a designated curb, often called the "kiss and fly" area. This prevents the need for parking and allows the traffic flow to continue smoothly.

Do not think that morning traffic issues are low on the priority lists of parents. At one focus group meeting I was conducting for a high school, we spent over half of our time on the parental frustrations with the morning traffic problems and safety concerns associated with it.

Morning traffic jams with busses and cars are a huge source of concern for most schools. Create a drop off area called the "kiss and learn" area. Using a bit of paint and maybe a few signs, designate a lane for those dropping off their students to enter and exit in an orderly fashion. If you have the space, a circle approach to this works wonders!

Inform parents and families by passing out flyers a few weeks before the launching of your new "kiss and learn" drop–off area. Share with them the safety benefits and time savings of this easy and organized way to drop off and pick up students.

Things to Do:

1. *Work with your central office buildings and grounds professionals to plan a "kiss and learn" drop–off/pick–up area.*
2. *Use paint (preferably a different color to denote the special space) and signs to direct parents and families use the new facility wisely.*
3. *Publicize the new area a few weeks before it goes into use. Explain the time–saving benefits, safety, and organization for all parents and families who drive their children to school.*
4. *Promote loving families with "kiss and learn"!*

23. Invite the Return

We can learn from professional marketers and salespeople, whose livelihood depends on repeat customers. Making sure customers know they are welcomed and encouraged to return is a cornerstone of successful business practice. Here is an example from my travels.

When I travel by plane, I park my car at an off–site parking facility. At my home airport, there are dozens of facilities all claiming to be the best, fastest, and least expensive way to park your car and get to your flight. Why do I keep going back to the same one when I have so many other options? Easy, they *ask* me to come back.

Upon my return, the shuttle–bus driver is always standing outside the door, rain or shine. Consistently, the driver asks if I had a good trip and welcomes me home. As the shuttle stops, the driver says, "Thank you. We look forward to seeing you on your next trip." By the time I get to the parking facility, my car is waiting and the lift gate is opened for me. As I step off the shuttle, another employee welcomes me home. This employee carries my luggage to my car, opens my door for me, and invites me back. I continue to choose this parking facility because they keep inviting me back!

Take the same approach with parents and guests to your school. Train all staff to say to someone leaving, "Thank you for visiting," "Come back again" or "When will we see you again?" Put up a few signs at the exits of your school that say, "Thanks for coming. See you next time." Always invite parents and families to return. This is a simple and effective way to let all families know they are welcome any time and, more importantly, that you are happy to see them.

Things to Do:

1. *Train all staff, including teachers, support staff, and clerical staff, to invite guests back to school any time they see one leaving.*
2. *Create signs that thank parents and families for coming and invite them back again.*

24. One Hundred Welcomes

Most schools have students whose first language is not English. I have visited schools where over sixty languages are spoken by students and, in one case, one hundred languages! How can we create a welcoming environment in a school where families speak one hundred languages? The answer: Create one hundred welcomes!

Start with a cross–curriculum meeting in your building. Create a project that allows students to research the word *welcome* in their native language. For those students who speak English as a first language, have them research the word in the language of their ancestors or pair them with bilingual students.

Students can create art posters with the greeting and include drawings that represent their native cultures. Once they are completed, hang the posters to create a "wall of welcome." Not only have you created a very welcoming environment, but you have connected it to student learning!

Things to Do:

1. *Plan a multi–disciplinary project that includes the study, spelling, and pronunciation of the word welcome in native languages or languages of ancestors.*

2. *Once the research is complete, have students create welcome signs as a visual arts project.*

3. *Find a wall that is clearly visible from the main entrance of your school. Post the welcome signs to create your "wall of welcome."*

4. *Change the displays as different grade levels or classes become involved in the project.*

5. *Invite parents and families to school to view their children's work and to feel welcome while doing so!*

25. Personal Greetings

Each morning at South Cobb High School, Dr. Grant Rivera and several of his staff members greet students being dropped off at school. They open car doors for students and peek into the car to say good morning to the driver and any other passengers. Students and families love the personal attention. The "we care" and "welcome" message is obvious.

By staying outside for ten minutes past the opening bell, Dr. Rivera discovered a hidden benefit. He has the opportunity to talk with students and families who are late and to suggest ways to avoid tardiness in the future. This personal attention to late arrivals has significantly reduced the problem and allowed Dr. Rivera the opportunity to interact with students and families. When frequently tardy students start arriving on time, Dr. Rivera reinforces this with praise for the student and appreciation for the family's assistance.

Things to Do:

1. *Schedule the staff duty roster to include some personal greeters during the morning arrival period.*
2. *Open car doors and welcome students to school. Thank families for their support for student success. Tell everyone to "make it a great day."*
3. *For those students who are late, take a minute or two to have a discussion with the parent and student. Create an "on–time" plan for the next day. When the tardy student arrives on time, be sure to reinforce this behavior by praising the student and thanking the family for their help.*

26. The Warm Transfer

Just about everyone can relate to the following experience: You call a business or agency with a problem. You explain the problem, only to discover that the person you are speaking with cannot help you. You are then transferred to someone else at which time you must repeat your problem. I think my personal record is explaining a problem to five different people before being connected to the right person. The solution is simple: Teach staff the concept of a warm transfer.

A warm transfer only requires that the caller share the problem *once*. If the person responding to the caller is not the appropriate staff member, that person places the caller on hold, finds the right staff member and shares the problem so the caller does not have to repeat themselves. The dialogue might look like this:

> "Mrs. Smith, I am going to place you on hold and find a person who can better help you."
> (Place caller on hold).
> "Mrs. Smith, I have Terry on the line." (Terry says hello). "I have explained your problem to her and she is ready to help you, OK?" (Caller agrees).
> "Mrs. Smith, it was a pleasure talking with you today. Is there anything else I can do for you before Terry takes over?"

At that point, Terry takes over the call and the customer is "warmly" transferred to the appropriate person.

I know of several schools, especially large secondary schools that have adapted the warm transfer process to rave reviews from parents.

Things to Do:

1. *Share the rationale for the warm transfer process with appropriate staff.*
2. *Collectively, have staff write a "script" that can be used each time a warm transfer is necessary.*
3. *Have appropriate staff practice the process on each other before taking it "live" with real calls.*
4. *Collect data from families about their experiences when contacting the school. Watch satisfaction rise!*

DOMAIN 2

TWO-WAY COMMUNICATION BETWEEN SCHOOL AND HOME

27. Honesty is Still the Best Policy

Many parents report that a serious concern to them is their perception that administrators and/or teachers are sometimes not completely honest and forthcoming in communicating with them. This issue, rooted in mismanaged and broken communication systems, can undo months, perhaps years, of efforts to build trusting relationships with parents. Any time a school employee is evasive or less than truthful about situations, the negative catalyst of disengagement is born. Parents and families usually interpret defensive postures taken by school personnel as evidence of guilt. Left unchecked, the result is devastating to school–family relationships.

If all educators will follow two simple rules, honest and trustful communication can be the cornerstone of the re–cultured school. 1) When employees of the school make an error, they should admit the mistake, discuss the resolution, and move on. 2) When employees of the school do not know an answer to a parent's question, they should offer to find the answer and get back to the parent as soon as possible.

These two simple rules can alter the course of communication. Teachers and administrators are human and are prone to make mistakes and errors in judgment. When parents become upset, the situation is usually compounded if staff members try to camouflage or minimize the problem in an effort to protect the school. If parents call with a concern, regardless of how small, it is never insignificant to them. If it were, they would not call.

Principals often present situations for which there are no easy solutions. The advice I give is simple. First, exhaust every avenue to determine the facts of the situation. Next, remind both the parent and the staff member that you were not present when the situation took place. Last, when there is no clear answer and there is a compelling argument on each side, my advice is always the same—err on the side of the child. If we value parents and families, there must be times when we support the notion that the staff member either misinterpreted a situation or is simply wrong.

Principals often continue to challenge this thinking by reminding me of teacher reactions to decisions that are seen as unsupportive of their efforts as teachers. There is a teachers think they are always "right," it is another clear signal that the culture of the organization is suffering. The moment disputes or disagreements are categorized as wins and losses, the essence of trustful relationships evaporates.

Things to Do:

1. *Adapt the two rules of good communication with all staff. Post them in teacher work areas.*
2. *Create a culture that is trusting, and when all else fails, err on the side of the child.*
3. *Log these types of events, and watch closely to see whether they decrease or increase.*
4. *Look for evidence of beliefs and values of staff in their daily actions and interactions with other colleagues, students, and families.*
5. *Adopt the "six month, two minute" business slogan when working with all parents and families.*

28. Family vs. Parent

Research teaches us that, when we use the word *parent*, we can potentially alienate up to 50 percent of adults who take charge of children's lives. Foster parents, grandparents, aunts, uncles, neighbors, group homes, temporary placements, and governmental agencies all play a role in shaping the lives of large numbers of children.

The word *family* covers every adult who enters the life of a child and cares for that child, whether it is on a permanent or temporary basis. Start all correspondences that are general in nature with the salutation: Dear (District or School Name) Families. It is warm, friendly, and to the point. It also ensures that all who read the letter know they are part of a family.

Things to Do:

1. *Review all correspondences (e.g., letters, advertisements, web pages, and newsletters) and replace the word parent/parents with family/ families.*

29. The Best Way to Communicate!

Schools are masterful at one–way communication. We send "stuff" home. We send so much stuff home that, unfortunately, our best intentions are woefully inadequate when communicating with families. Most schools send "too much stuff" home. As a result, many families do not read, process, or understand much of the information they receive. Successful communication includes verification that the family received and understood the information. Often, we do not follow up to determine whether the information we sent was received and understood.

A principal once told me at the end of a workshop that his school already had good two–way communication in place. He said, "Anything that is important requires that a parent sign it and return it. Then we know the message and information were received."

"Not necessarily," I responded. Unfortunately, we all lead busy lives. Our children have a way of capitalizing on the crowded agendas we have as parents. They learn at an early age to wait as long as possible and then, just before a signature is needed, to pull the document from a backpack and utter the phrase, "I need this signed." Families, already pressed for time, quickly move to a fall back position. They ask their child to explain what the paper is all about. Usually, the answer is something to the effect of, "Oh, it's just some thing for the thing we did that the teacher wants . . . no big deal." The parent, not wanting his or her child to be late with the return of the paper, signs it in good faith. This action usually does not present too much of a problem, except when the school assumes it has communicated.

Case in point: Research from the U.S. Department of Education ("Strong Families, Strong Schools," 1994) indicated that 48 percent of ninth grade parents did not help their child select classes or helped only once. Yet, if one were to check with the guidance counselors at the school, they could produce a schedule proposal that contained a parent signature for each student. Did communication really take place here? Probably not.

The first step in improving communication between school and family is for the school to determine exactly how to communicate with the family via telephones, technology, faxes, high–speed printers, on-line postage services, instant messaging, voice–mail, and other communication avenues open to us. Simply put: *Ask them*. Ask parents to let you know the best way to contact them. Once you have this information, be sure to contact them in the manner that is most convenient to them. Many schools believe that sending an e–mail may be the best, fastest, and most inexpensive way to communicate. While I do not argue that it is fast and inexpensive, it may not be the best way to communicate with all families.

Technology allows us to find the best way to communicate or to communicate in multiple ways. Some technology will allow you to code the manner of communication into it so that it will automatically dial a telephone number, send an e–mail, print out a letter for mailing, or all three! When you ask parents and families how best to communicate with them, you are sending a clear message that you value them, their children, and their time.

Things to Do:

1. *Survey parents to determine the best way to communicate with them.*
2. *Investigate technology that can assist you with communication.*
3. *Log communication efforts and spot check with parents and families to determine rate of message and information receipt.*
4. *Create systems to determine whether communication is understood.*

30. Keep it Informal at First

The majority of interactions between families and school personnel happen at school functions. Most families who are disengaged from the school do not attend these types of events. Taking an inventory of families who attend school events reveals that the families either are tied to the event due to the participation of their child (sports, music, and so on) or are already engaged and always attend general school functions. In order to best cultivate relationships with disengaged families, school personnel should first concentrate on building relationships with those families through informal channels.

Superintendents and principals working in smaller towns and villages across the United States report that a visit to the local supermarket can initiate numerous informal and impromptu discussions with parents and community members. The size of the town and the limited access to certain public venues increases the likelihood that school officials will mingle with parents and families in informal ways.

School leaders in larger, more metropolitan areas can replicate such informal meetings with parents by creating avenues for informal discussions. Principals can make themselves available at the local coffee shop or restaurant once or twice a month and let the public know that the availability is to create informal discussions and build relationships. Neighborhood meetings in the homes of families are also a small and intimate way to connect with families. A host family can invite neighbors whose children attend the school for an hour or so of conversation with the principal. There no need for a set agenda or handouts, just the ability for parents and families to talk directly to the principal.

Each year, Dr. Bob Hassler, Superintendent of North Penn School District in Lansdale, Pennsylvania, has a series of community conversations, which any community member can attend to have an informal conversation with the superintendent. These informal conversations are beneficial for all involved.

In addition to attending school–sponsored events, principals are encouraged to attend one or two major community events so that the public may see the principal in a different light. Whether it is the annual Fourth of July fireworks display or a fall apple festival, just a few hours of time will set the stage for numerous future relationships.

Things to Do:

1. *Target neighborhoods where family engagement is minimal. Create opportunities either through local establishments or in private homes to meet and talk informally with parents.*
2. *Select one or two high–profile community events to attend.*
3. *Track discussions and follow–up on new relationships. Work to increase relationships in particular neighborhoods by reasonable percentages.*

31. Open Unless We're Closed

I was visiting a high school principal friend of mine at about 5:00 p.m., which is after the school offices are closed. I knew the principal was still in the building because we had an appointment. As I walked from my car to the entrance, another car pulled up, and out came a mother of a graduating senior. She was distraught and mistook me for a staff member. She began to explain that her son was not graduating and she did not understand why. She said, "I was hoping to catch somebody here at school so I could talk to them. I got out of work early hoping someone would be here."

This parent really was not sure whether the school office was open or closed. She was taking a chance, and she knew it. I alerted the principal, and he met with the parent immediately. Most schools do not function on the same calendar or clock hours as the business world. Many parents assume that because they work until five or six in the evening, that the school offices and personnel are working as well. Parents often find the doors locked when they stop by after their workday. If there are no clear office and personnel hours published and posted, this situation can be frustrating to parents and can result in a negative catalyst leading to disengagement.

In every newsletter and on every informational document, include the office hours for all parents and families. Post signs in the front of the building with the departmental office hours, not just the main office hours. Do all you can to help people know what time offices open and what time they close.

We want families to know our hours as instinctively as you know the hours to your favorites stores. Think about it. What do the stores do to communicate their hours? When you answer that question, do the same thing.

Things to do:

1. *Determine the best ways in which to share continuously office and school building hours of operation with parents and families.*
2. *Determine whether you have the capability to allow someone to work a flexible shift, thus providing some coverage in the late afternoon for parent visits or concerns.*
3. *Survey parents to determine the best times for school visits.*

4. *Repeatedly publish and post hours of operation.*
5. *Repeatedly publish and post emergency and after–hour phone numbers.*

32. Untangle the Web

Several years ago, I had the privilege of being involved in a national grant and research program called *The Bridge Project*. *The Bridge Project* was constructed around the concept of using technology (at that time voice–mail) to help schools and families connect and be involved with each other. The premise was simple. Teachers left messages of daily activities in school, and parents could call in and listen to those messages, affording them the opportunity to stay connected with school activities, academics, homework, and teacher expectations.

What had been evident in prior parent–involvement research and in this project was that family usage of technology drops in direct proportion to timeliness and relevance of the information being shared.[6] This fundamental concept still holds true today, even as technology has evolved. Web–based and telephone–based information systems can be a tremendous asset to schools, or they can be huge liabilities depending on the updating, refreshing, and quality of information available to parents.

Most frequently cited by parents are school Web sites and the degree to which information is old or not relevant.

Things to Do:

1. *Create, re–create, and update your Web site and other technology used to communicate and engage with parents.*
2. *Develop a plan to monitor updating.*
3. *Survey parents often as to the effectiveness of the technology being used. Respond accordingly.*
4. *Read Web site usage reports to determine the effectiveness of your Web site and to monitor visits.*

6   Bauch, J. P. (2000). *Electronic parent involvement? New developments with phones, e–mail, and the Internet to link schools and homes.* Paper presented at the 10th annual international roundtable on School, Family, and Community Partnerships. New Orleans, LA.

33. Newsletters that Link Families to Learning

Dr. Karen Mapp, Lecturer at the Harvard Graduate School of Education, often talks about taking every communication opportunity and linking it to learning. The monthly newsletter is a staple for just about every school. Usually, these newsletters are long and filled with very important information that, unfortunately, is never read. In working with parents, we discovered that most are either overwhelmed by the amount of information or do not find the newsletters significant or relevant. Most newsletters contain information about honor rolls, awards, programs, the library, the PTO, fundraising, sports, activities, and academics. The traditional "letter from the principal" usually appears on the first page and often reiterates most of the information found in the newsletter.

Parents and families become immune to overloaded newsletters and can even become disenfranchised from the school through the newsletter itself. For example, front–page stories of scholarship winners and honor roll students can be disheartening to those families whose children are not academically proficient. The subconscious message these features send to them reinforces their belief that the school does not support all students and families. Even though the principal's message is important to the principal, there is no rule that says it needs to be on page one. Principals can either use the column to support learning at home or simply move it off the front page.

Even better is the idea of breaking apart the newsletter so that it is not large and unmanageable. For example, in Canandaigua, New York, parent volunteers come into the schools once a month and put together a "newsletter" comprised of flyers and announcements from parent and student clubs and organizations. The school newsletter is then more concise, is focused on academics, and is more of a support for home learning. Parents who want to read the "extra news" can, but all parents receive a relevant newsletter that is meaningful to them.

Other schools, such as some elementary schools in Hickman County, Tennessee, send weekly classroom newsletters. Parents have formed a positive habit of reading the newsletter in which the teacher not only reports class activities, both past and future, but shares insights for parents on how to support learning at home. Teachers using this approach report that most parents are involved and engaged in classroom academics and activities.

Things to Do:

1. *Review your newsletters for length, content, and relevance to all parents.*
2. *Survey family opinions of newsletter communication, and survey again after changes are made based on those opinions. Record the differences in survey opinions.*
3. *Set goals for communication satisfaction through newsletters.*
4. *Have home support for student learning as a focus to your newsletter.*

34. Banish the Guardian from the Kingdom

At some point in the history of education, we decided that we needed to maintain a level of political correctness and not refer to every adult as a parent. Thus was born the phrase, "Dear Parent/Guardian." The overuse of this phrase, coupled with the present culture of "we know best" found in many schools, sends a negative message to adults receiving this information. The salutation is cold, impersonal, and reinforces to families that we care little about them or their children. It is akin to receiving mail that is addressed to "occupant." The phrase is used in letters, newsletters, permission slips, and under every line dedicated to an adult signature.

Things to Do:

1. *Collect every document that has the word guardian on it and revise it to include the word family or families.*
2. *Check with school attorneys for language that can be used on official documents, such as medical forms and field trip request forms.*
3. *Consider everyone as part of your school family.*

35. Translation, Translation, Translation

Translation is a critically important first step in communicating proactively with families of different cultural origins. While being culturally sensitive should not end with translation, the ability to communicate with all cultures is of great importance as a first step toward building positive relationships.

Native speakers of the language provide the best translations. Often, acquired language is more formal than the language spoken in neighborhoods that surround your school. Translate into the informal dialects that are spoken so that messages from the school can be understood and comprehended.

Formal translation done by computers or software programs continues to be the least desirable manner in which to translate. Programs can often confuse verb tense, masculine and feminine use of languages, and other grammatical elements. There are numerous stories of well–intentioned schools distributing software–developed translations and causing a disaster. One such story is my own. A newsletter went out inviting parents to allow their children to attend the "alcohol and drug free" all–night after–prom party. Unfortunately, due to a slight shift in adjectives, Latino families received a letter that invited them to allow their children to "attend an all night party where alcohol and drugs would be served." Do yourself a favor and work with a native speaker who can translate appropriately. Your phone will ring less, and families will appreciate it.

Things to Do:

1. *Determine the informal languages in your community.*
2. *Check with your local churches and businesses to learn about translation services and possibly join forces in the need for translation.*
3. *Seek family and community volunteers who can translate information so that all families can be connected to the school.*
4. *Survey non–English or limited English families to determine their level of satisfaction with your efforts. Set targets for improved satisfaction among these families.*

36. Bring School to Families . . . on a Bus!

Several years ago, I spoke and worked with the schools in Hillsborough County, Florida. At that time, the county parent involvement coordinator was Judy Dato. Judy was a dynamo with parent and family engagement and was nationally known for her work and writing on the subject. The first time I met Judy, she said, "Would you like to see my bus?"

Judy took me to see "her bus," a reconditioned city bus repainted and spruced up like a brand new coach. "Hillsborough County Public Schools Parent Involvement Bus," was painted in large letters on the side of the bus. The interior had been gutted and refitted as a traveling classroom. There were computers, books, tapes, pamphlets, and information that parents and families needed. In the rear of the bus was a comfortable space designed for meeting with parents who were unable to travel to their children's school.

The bus was so popular that neighborhoods scheduled it months in advance. When the Parent Involvement Bus arrived, families would line up to visit the bus, meet school district staff, and get answers to common questions. The bus took the fear out of going to the school for many parents. The bus also took outreach by schools to a new level.

About a year later, I mentioned this bus to Kim Bauerle, whose superintendent Dr. Jan Billings (Anaheim, California, now retired), was supportive of family engagement. Jan sent Kim to Tampa, Florida, to research the Parent Involvement Bus project. Kim returned with reports, diagrams, and pictures. Local business partnerships and grant funding were needed for both the Hillsborough Bus and the Anaheim Project. Jan and Kim worked tirelessly to solicit funding and sell the Parent Involvement Bus to the community of Anaheim.

About a year later, I spoke at the Orange County Conference for Human Services. Jan Billings met me at the door, and I experienced a sense of déjà vu!

"Come here! Let me show you my bus!" Jan led me to the door and the new Anaheim Union High School District Parent Involvement Bus rolled into place. I was lucky to be one of the first people to board the bus and see what vision, ingenuity, and a little arm twisting would accomplish. The bus was magnificent!

Today, you can visit either school district, and if you can catch it, you can see the parent involvement bus rolling through neighborhoods bringing education and hope to thousands of families. It will inspire you.

Things to Do:

1. *Visit Hillsborough or Anaheim and see one or both of the busses!*
2. *Work with your school district, community, businesses, and grant writers to formulate a grant to fund a family–involvement bus project.*
3. *Keep your effort and attitude high. It won't be easy.*

37. Rules of Communication: *The Rule of Sevens and Negative 4X*

For those of you who are reading this and are looking for a solid research article to fall back on, there isn't one. This is my own theory based on my personal experience. *The Rule of Sevens and Negative 4X* refers to the way comments and information spread through the community in a very short amount of time.

While writing this book, I ruptured a calf muscle in my right leg. I didn't go to the doctor right away, but called a friend and described my symptoms. He encouraged me to go to the doctor. This phone call took place on a Monday evening at about ten o'clock. The events that followed illustrate *The Rule of Sevens and Negative 4X*.

By six o'clock on Tuesday evening, fifteen people knew of my injury and were contacting me by either phone or e-mail to see how I was doing. Eighteen hours earlier, three people—my wife, the friend I called, and I—knew of my injury, and now fifteen knew. By Wednesday evening, another seven people joined the group. (Twenty-two people if you stopped counting.) I was amazed that word had traveled so far and so fast. People from other states, clients, friends, associates, and former customers were now hearing about my ruptured calf muscle!

People I had personally told of my injury:

1. My wife
2. The friend I phoned
3. The vice president of Family Friendly Schools
4. The operations' director of Family Friendly Schools
5. A customer on the west coast
6. The Fed Ex guy
7. My brother

Wow! That is seven people! The rule works. *The Rule of Sevens* indicates that when we, as humans, have a significant experience, either positive or negative, we will tell seven people within 24 hours. Without thinking much about it, I told exactly seven people within 24 hours. (I never claimed that this is scientific.)

Now the test was to see whether the second part of the rule worked, *The Rule of Negative 4X*. This rule states that human beings spread negative information four times faster than positive information. Even though you would think I had better things to do, I sat down, investigated, and diagramed exactly how the information about my unfortunate accident spread. (I eliminated names to protect the guilty!)

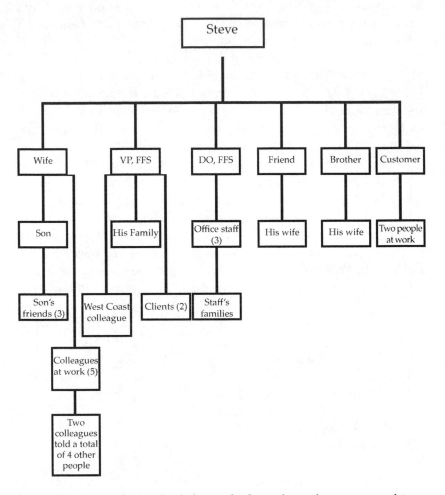

For those of you who have studied my chart, there are two things that will become very clear:

1. Thirty–six people, over five times the original number who heard the news directly from me, knew of my accident within twenty–four hours. (I only counted those that I could actually track and verify.

2. I **<u>DID NOT</u>** tell my mother!

This humorous look at communication can also apply to schools. School employees have to work four times harder at getting "good" news out into the public. Unfortunately, the bad news takes care of itself. Learn to control how news spreads and establish a protocol so that *The Rule of Sevens and Negative 4X* work in your favor.

Things to Do:

1. *Teach staff The Rule of Sevens and Negative 4X. Explain how comments and information spread through the community in a very short amount of time.*
2. *Work to provide "good" news and apply the rules to those pieces of news that are beneficial to the school.*
3. *Increase the effort to encourage the dissemination of good news as opposed to negative news.*
4. *Test the rules by sharing information and then tracking its progress through different people.*

38. A Blast of Good News

Technology provides a low–maintenance medium for communicating with students, families, and stakeholders. Use this online medium to minimize expenses incurred by hard–copy documents, and to maximize two–way communication. To be effective, determine with a survey or other means of collecting information how many families have access to e–mail and inform all families of the numerous free, Web–based e–mail programs that are available.

Technology–savvy staff members can assist in creating a master database with fields that allow for tailored communication. Examples include e–mails sent by grade level, extracurricular club/organization, athletic team, and academic department.

Things to Do:

1. *Encourage every teacher to request e–mail addresses from every student. This process can be encouraged through a standard form used in every office and by every teacher that asks families to provide updated contact information at every home–school interaction (parent meetings, attendance office, open house, athletic events, and other events).*
2. *Create a database for e–mail addresses that sorts families and students by specific fields for more effective and tailored communication.*
   a. *Grade level (Example: E–mail all families of ninth–grade students to invite them to ninth–grade advisement)*
   b. *Athletic and/or extracurricular participation (Example: Invitation to sports banquet)*
   c. *Families of non–native speakers (Example: Families who prefer to receive Spanish translation of e–mail)*
3. *Include additional stakeholders in the e–mail blast. Examples include Partners in Education, prominent businesses and political figures, and alumni.*
4. *Take every opportunity to personalize the e–mail so that it serves as informational, invitational, and engaging.*
5. *Include personal messages from the principal, student success stories, or student autobiographies. Keep it simple, yet personal.*

39. What's on the Fridge?

Refrigerator magnets provide a cost effective strategy to remind families of important dates and school contact information. The following types of information might be included on your magnets:

- Dates—end of grading period, open house, conference week, student holidays, school–wide celebrations, etc.
- Contact Information—school phone number, Web site, school bus transportation office, names of grade level counselors and administrators (if applicable)
- School mission/beliefs (Jones Middle School – Striving to be a Family Friendly School)

Things to Do:

1. *Determine dates and contact information that are closely linked to family engagement.*
2. *Purchase the largest, most colorful magnets you can afford.*
3. *Distribute to families at every opportunity—open house events, athletic events, through local businesses.*
4. *Print magnets in multiple languages to assist families of non–English speakers.*

40. Adding the Personal Touch

Most schools publicize school events in a variety of ways. These might include newsletter announcements, e–mail blasts, Web site notices, roadside marquees, and automated phone calls. Despite such efforts, some families still will not receive the information.

Consider adding a personal touch by making a personal call to each family to confirm they are aware and planning to attend the special activity. Often high school students need community service hours and would be willing to assist with these calls. Give these students a script and the contact information for all the families invited to the event. Students could follow this actual ninth–grade script to improve two–way communication.

> *Student: "Hello, my name is Jane and I am a student at Jones High School. I am calling to make sure your family is planning to attend ninth grade advisement in February. This meeting is important because the teachers and counselors will be helping your child develop a graduation plan. Did you receive the letter from the school with the detailed information?"*
>
> *If the answer is yes, then the student responds, "Great, we look forward to seeing you."*
>
> *If the answer is no, then the student responds, "I will ask a staff member to call you back and explain the details so you can make arrangements to attend. When would it be convenient for one of our staff members to contact you?"*

Things to Do:

1. *Plan accordingly. Determine the number of families to be called, number of volunteers needed, and number of accessible phone lines, and then work backwards to allow adequate time to reach all families. Note: If you are using students to make phone calls, the purpose should be to confirm receipt of initial correspondence (letter, e–mail, or other correspondence, detailing time, place, and purpose of event), not to discuss any student specific information.*

2. *Identify groups of students who have the phone etiquette and maturity to assist in calling families. Make the calls after school.*

3. *Type a script. (As the language skills of the volunteers permit, identify students who can speak to families in their native languages.)*

4. *Print contact information for all students involved with the event (all ninth graders, all students in a particular class).*
5. *Designate a staff member who will make follow—up calls when families have questions not suitable for a student volunteer.*

41. Bilingual Persons: Specific Points of Contact

All families want to be involved in and support their children's education. As a veteran educator who has observed thousands of schools and interacted with countless families, I have never met a parent or family member who did not want his or her child to be successful in school. Despite the best of intentions, various barriers often contribute to disengagement between a family and their child's academic success. An example of such a barrier is the inability of non–English speakers to navigate the waters of public schools. The language barrier often contributes directly to their disengagement.

Identify specific bilingual individuals in the building who can serve as a safe, familiar point of contact for native speakers. For example, in one high school, two teachers are identified as "Friendly for Hispanic/Latino Families" and two additional staff members serve as "Friendly for Serbian Families."

Front office personnel and families know in advance that these teachers are available to assist when needed. Teacher names, phone numbers, and e–mail addresses are available on cards in the office and throughout the building for families who wish to contact a staff member who can communicate in the family's native language. We print each card in the respective language with a brief explanation of our appreciation for their involvement and suggestions of ways to support their child's success.

These bilingual staff members also can serve as staff development trainers to help their coworkers understand cultural and linguistic differences. They can facilitate and compliment the efforts of all staff members to communicate with multi–cultural families.

Things to Do:

1. *Identify the different languages spoken by students and their families within the school.*
2. *Identify staff members who can assist in communicating with these families. Caution: Be sure to determine which staff members have strengths in the written and spoken language. For example, some non–native speakers may wish not to do written translation but may be proficient in verbal skills. Do not set up a staff member to struggle or feel inadequate!*

3. *Publicize on the Web site, in newsletters, and within the school (on business cards in the counseling officers, attendance office, etc.) internal staff who can serve as a point of contact for non–English speakers. Examples of invitational, culturally–specific engagement strategies include the following:*

   a. *Get multiple translations that say, "Can we help your family? Feel free to contact Ms. Jones, native Spanish speaker, should you have questions about school and your child's success. Your family is important. (Alex.jones@school.com phone number)"*

42. Got Questions?

How often have you walked into a government office or stumbled across a Web site with a specific question or need and been unable to find the answer or help you desired? In school buildings and on Web sites, families should not feel like a mouse in a maze. This type of wandering creates frustration and confusion that undermines family engagement and creates strained relationships prior to the first person–to–person contact. Create a "help desk" in your building and on your Web site that allows general questions to receive specific answers.

Within the school building, this may be as simple as a sign that says, "How can we help you? Families and guests are welcome to come to the front office for assistance." A secretary or student aide can provide specific assistance from this point.

For families who prefer the convenience of online information, establish a link on the school Web site that allows for general inquires. The inquiry form should include "guide fields" for the family to indicate the area they need information about, such as academics, athletics, extra–curricular activities, or community information. In addition, the form requests identifying information (student name, grade level, family contact information), and provides a comment box for specific questions. The secretary or webmaster who receives the web inquiry is then able to route the request to the appropriate staff member.

Things to Do:
Front Office Help Desk
1. *Place a sign near the front entrance that directs visitors to the front office or help desk.*
   a. *Consider placing a similar sign in the parking lot and inside the front doors.*
2. *Train the person at the "help desk" in customer service.*

Web Site Help Desk
1. *Request the webmaster to create a mailbox to receive general inquiries.*
   a. *If financial resources permit, follow the example provided above with guide fields and a comment box. Identify one staff member who will check the link each day and route inquiries to the appropriate persons.*

b. *If financial resources do not permit Web site upgrades, identify one e–mail address to which families can e–mail inquiries.*

43. Families as Cultural Translators

We need the best information we can get in order to work limited English families. Usually, we rely on reading, research, and experts in the field to help us to connect with these families. Often, we overlook the most valuable resource available—the families themselves. Much research points to the role of families as translators of their own cultures. There is no better manner in which to glean important information about children than to ask their families. This concept, taken a step further, will provide the school with another avenue to learn the cultural nuances of families from other countries.

Invite family members to teach the school staff. At first, they may be reluctant to become a speaker for teachers. The best way to begin this process is to start small, perhaps just a few teachers and the parent in an informal setting. Once the parent is comfortable sharing with a small group, he or she may be willing to speak to the entire staff. Allowing families to share their culture not only helps us as educators meet the needs of our ever–changing student populations, but also sends a clear message to families that we care deeply about them, their culture, and their children.

Things to Do:

1. *Find limited or non–English speaking families who would be willing to share important information about their culture.*
2. *Inform families that the purpose is to help the staff understand the family's native culture. Share the information that you would like to understand better.*
3. *Start with a small, informal group of teachers to build the confidence of the family member.*
4. *Have a translator, preferably a non–staff member, on hand to assist if English is a problem. Inform the family member that a translator will be there to help.*
5. *Once the family member is more confident, increase the size of the group or expand the program to other topics or parents.*
6. *Deliver the clear impression that the families' knowledge is needed and appreciated within the school.*

44. Let Students Be the Pathway to Engaging All Families

Engaging the disenfranchised family calls for many different creative approaches to collect much needed information about their needs and challenges. We know from research that the best and most effective way to build relationships with traditionally disengaged families is to make the effort to reach out and understand, appreciate, and value both their culture and characteristics. Teachers can teach more effectively when they can obtain information about their students' home environment. A simple and effective way to garner information about families, their cultures, beliefs, values, and attitudes is to have students participate in a student autobiography project.

Students sharing information about themselves, their home, their families, and—in the cases of limited or non–English speaking students—their country of origin will go a long way toward building relationships with all families, especially those who have traditionally been difficult to reach. Teachers can use this project as a way to engage families with their children. Structure the autobiography project so that students must interview their family in order to gain the necessary knowledge to complete the project. Be creative with the final products. Use three–sided boards and bulletin boards to display the results of the student autobiography project. If possible, acquire disposable cameras and ask students to have their pictures taken with their families, siblings, favorite pets, neighborhood friends, and extended family members. At the conclusion, invite all the families to see the completed projects and to celebrate the success.

Things to Do:

1. *Look at curriculum sequence and planning to determine where best a student autobiography project would fit.*
2. *Schedule the project as early in the year as possible.*
3. *Follow up with teachers about what they learned from the autobiographies and how best to use the information to build effective relationships with all families.*
4. *Use the experience to celebrate student accomplishments with all families.*

45. Info@

Technology provides a wonderful vehicle for two–way communication. School Web sites and voice–mail systems are excellent tools to help foster better communication between home and school.

The "info@" feature of a Web site is an excellent idea to let anyone who has a question or concern share it with you. Parents, families, and community members can all use the "info@" button to ask questions, offer suggestions, register concerns, or simply communicate.

When visitors click the "info@" button, they should see an information screen that asks for the following information. To avoid anonymous communication, require completion of these fields.

1. Name
2. E–mail address
3. Nature of communication
   (question, comment, complaint, suggestion)
4. Space for the specific question, comment, complaint, suggestion
5. Preferred method of response (e–mail, phone call)
6. Phone number

Set the Web site to generate an automatic return e–mail when the person hits the send button.

Thank you for using "info@_____." We value your input. Your question or comment is being routed to the person who can best respond to you. You will receive a response in the manner you chose within twenty–four hours. Please contact us any time either by using this service or by calling us at XXX–XXXX.

A similar feature exists with your school voice–mail system. Publicize a phone number and/or a mailbox number that parents and families can call to leave a message with a question, concern, or comment about any facet of your school. If possible, direct the caller to press the pound (#) sign when the call is completed. At that point, a prerecorded message can play, providing the same information contained in the above referenced e–mail.

Things to Do:

1. *Discuss with your technology staff the possibility of creating an "info@" link from the main page of your Web site.*
2. *Create the link as stated above.*
3. *Investigate the opportunity to provide the same service with your present voice–mail system.*
4. *Assign someone on the staff the task of collecting the information and directing it to the appropriate personnel for response.*
5. *Answer all questions, concerns, and comments within twenty–four hours.*

46. Conduct the *Things to Know* Exercise

The lack of opportunity to share ideas, concerns, or suggestions directly with school staff frustrates families. The same frustration exists within the staff. A wonderful exercise to promote healthy, two–way communication is the "things to know" exercise.

Create opportunities for school staff and families to be together. First, separate the teaching staff from families. Using chart paper and markers, invite both groups to write things they would like the other group to know but do not often get the opportunity to share. Explain to both groups that this is an opportunity both groups desire. When complete, collect the charts, mix them up, and post them in the room. Invite everyone to reconvene after reviewing the charts for content.

Often the ideas and comments are very similar, regardless of whether a family member or staff member wrote them. Common themes of care and concern will emerge. Use the comments as springboards for discussions and plans to enhance communication with families. If it is impossible to bring groups of parents and teachers together, create the charts separately and publish them to both groups. This activity promotes effective dialog and two–way communication when, through a process of discovery, everyone realizes they want the same thing, success for the child.

Things to Do:

1. *Acquire chart paper and markers.*
2. *Bring staff and families together by scheduling meetings and events both on and off school property.*
3. *Follow the "things to know" process outlined above.*
4. *Post the charts in random order and share the information with all participants.*
5. *Lead a discussion in determining similarities and differences from the charts. Are there themes that emerge?*
6. *Use this information as a springboard for discussion and future communication.*

47. Different Communication

It is a privilege for me to travel the country and work with thousands of teachers. I enjoy interacting with teachers and listening to their hopes, dreams, and fears. One consistent message from teachers about communication is the fear of not being able to handle different families and situations. (I like the word *different* better than *difficult*.)

Administrators tend to assume that, because teachers are so tremendously skilled in communicating with students all day long, that communication ability transcends to communicating with parents and families. It is not necessarily true. Many teachers feel they lack the skills necessary to communicate effectively with all parents and families, especially in situations that become difficult.

A teacher in a workshop shared a concern echoed numerous times in my travels. She said, "If I try to call all my parents, inevitably they want to keep me on the phone for twenty or thirty minutes. I just do not have that kind of time." It is easy to remedy this legitimate concern. Teachers can simply say, "I am calling all of my parents tonight to let them know the great things that are happening. It sounds like you and I need more time to talk. Could we continue this conversation on/at _____? I really appreciate your understanding. I will call you back on _____ at _____, okay?"

This simple little technique works for most instances when families want to take a greater amount of time than is available. Unfortunately, administrators assume that teachers instinctively have the ability to handle all types of communication. More staff development time and resources need to be devoted to helping teachers effectively communicate with all families.

Things to Do:

1. *Be aware that school staff members may need assistance in communicating with all families.*
2. *Dedicate staff development time and resources to enhance and practice effective communication skills.*

48. A Remedy for "Education–ese"

Consider the following paragraph from a school pamphlet on attendance and tardy procedures:

> At _____ School, we hold attendance and punctuality to class as a fundamental priority in providing a sound educational experience for all inhabitants of our school. The OAT is responsible for processing all attendance and tardiness issues. Students, parents, and guardians are responsible for directing such issues to OAT. Both habitual and unusual or catastrophic circumstances can all be effectively monitored and processed through OAT..."

First, what is OAT? (I later found it was the acronym for the Office of Attendance and Tardies...good grief!) While I am sure there are many families who can decipher this diatribe of directions, how about changing the language to something like this:

> We care greatly for all of our students and families. Mr. Smith and Mrs. Jones will handle attendance and tardiness issues. The attendance office is located next to the cafeteria. The phone number for the office is _____, and to e–mail the office, use attendance@school.com. We want to see you every day! It's not the same without you!

As you look at all of the written communication that you provide families, look for the formality of the language and the use of educational acronyms or labels that might be obvious to us but foreign to families.

PS: As a rule, there is never a reason to use the word *facilitate*!

Things to Do:

1. *Collect one copy of every document, pamphlet, booklet, or other material that is created for families.*
2. *Form a communications committee that oversees the language used when communicating with families.*
3. *As revisions are needed, work toward simple, straightforward,*

and welcoming language for families. Avoid acronyms or use of educational terms that are probably unfamiliar to families.

4. All written contact with families should be reviewed by the communication committee and receive its seal of approval. Get a "Family Friendly Approved" stamp!

49. Family Bulletin Boards

If your school has a family center, parents and families understand this is a great place in which to communicate with each other and share ideas, information, and knowledge about upcoming activities and events. We strongly encourage you to consider opening a family center. However, space limitations and shrinking budgets often do not allow schools the luxury of family centers. Parents and families still need an opportunity to communicate with each other, so give them their own bulletin board.

Work with your school parent–teacher group to locate and design an effective bulletin board. It should be displayed close to a main entrance of your school. Create different areas on the board, such as a monthly calendar, testing information, and general information about the school. Consider different languages spoken by parents and families. You may even want to give families a community space where they can advertise events in their neighborhoods, babysitting, rides to meetings, or other shared concerns. Create pockets for documents like "How to Survive Math" and "What is a Standard?" Assign a task force, usually within the parent–teacher organization, to keep the board current and stocked with handouts and informational flyers.

Knapp Elementary School, part of the North Penn School District, takes this idea a step further. To accommodate the needs of all parents, Knapp's family bulletin board is actually three bulletin boards presented in three different languages. Students assist by creating the flags of the representative countries. The flags are then used as backdrops on the bulletin boards. Parents and families can easily identify the correct board by the flag of their country of origin. This trilingual approach has significantly improved parent and family communication.

Ensure that no other organization encroaches on the bulletin board. Only parents and families can post information. Should teachers want to share information with families, instruct them to go through the parent–teacher organization to have their information posted.

Things to Do:

1. Purchase a large bulletin board or devote an existing bulletin board to families and community information.
2. Work with the parent–teacher organization to set up the board and the guidelines for use.
3. Help the parent–teacher group create a process to maintain the bulletin board.
4. Inform all parents and families that they have their very own bulletin board for their use. Publicize the board as often as possible.

50. Fingers Can Still Walk

Every day, week, or month, I pick up my favorite newspaper or magazine and read the same advertisements with the same information and the same phone numbers. I also know that I can let my "fingers do the walking" and search my yellow pages for services that I might require. In both cases, the contact information that I need is constantly and consistently presented to me. Schools should get in the habit of doing the same thing. Giving information once, usually at the beginning of the year, is not going to go a long way to promote healthy communication.

Just about every American leads a hectic and busy life. If we are committed to establishing positive, two–way communication, the foundation of that communication must be the repeated publishing and advertising of important phone numbers, Web site addresses, and e–mail addresses. Create documents that have pertinent information and share them in the community. Work with local retail managers for availability in their stores and place them in doctors' offices. I know of one story in which the local supermarket asked customers whether they had a child in the local school. If customers said, "Yes," the cashier dropped a phone number and e–mail card in their shopping bags.

Every document published should include school contact information. All important phone numbers and e–mail addresses should be on your school Web site in a "contact us" or "contact your child's teacher" section. Using community groups, businesses, and agencies as communication ambassadors will increase the information flow and help all families communicate with their children's schools.

If you have a large limited–English or non–English speaking population, consider translating the information and having it available at community centers, churches, and businesses that specialize in working with families of differing cultures. Perhaps an ethnically based grocery store is popular with a particular segment of families. Ask the local manager if he will display school contact information so that all parents can easily communicate with the school. Most will be happy to help.

Things to Do:

1. Publish accurate and up–to–date lists of phone numbers and e–mails for all administration and staff.
2. Through the communications committee, distribute the information throughout the community.
3. Work with the technology staff to ensure there is a "contact" link on the main page of your school Web site.
4. Consider this information as a continuous flow, not a one–time event.

51. Signs, Signs . . . Everywhere a Sign

For selected school events that apply to all students and families, consider placing signs in the community along major roadways and intersections. Consider the effectiveness of real estate signs in promoting a neighborhood or home for sale. Much like the local realtor, schools can publicize school events to motorists. This strategy is particularly effective during summer months when parents and students may be less inclined to check a school Web site or drive by the school marquee.

Depending on financial resources, schools can inexpensively purchase blank real estate signs and stands from a hardware store or request donations from a host of local realtors. Recycle signs year after year by simply changing the date of an open house, conference week, back–to–school kickoff, or other event.

Things to Do:

1. *Gather materials—blank signs, and plastic letters or stencils.*
2. *Remember that less is more to a motorist speeding down the roadway: Keep the message and lettering clear and concise.*
3. *Determine locations that will provide the greatest exposure to major roadways and intersections, at the local park, and near the entrance of a prominent business.*
4. *Do not be so proud of the signage that you fail to pick up the signs immediately following the event! Do not create the impression that a school's signage in the community is outdated or irrelevant. You do not want a family to ignore the next sign!*

DOMAIN 3

INCREASED DEGREE OF ENGAGEMENT

52. Set the Vision: Create a Family Engagement Policy

Having a policy for family engagement at the district level will strengthen the consistency and continuity of family engagement throughout the school district. However, even if your school district does not have a policy, or the policy in place is somewhat nebulous, individual schools can still create meaningful and real policies from which to create goals and action plans. Mr. John O'Meara, Principal of Yea High School in Yea, Victoria, and Australia did just that. I first met John when he attended a Family Friendly Schools Conference in the fall of 2006. Shortly afterward, John shared the following process and policy with me:

> Yea High School is a co–educational secondary college of three hundred fifty students situated one hundred kilometers [approximately sixty–two miles] northeast of Melbourne [Australia] and provides for the educational needs of a mixture of rural and semi–rural communities. The school has over 40 percent of its students traveling up to fifty kilometers [approximately thirty–one miles] to school by bus.
>
> I had been grappling with the need for our school to be more connected to our parent population. I had heard about this concept of "Family Friendly Schools" when I visited Alaska in the summer of 2005. When I returned, I started to research this concept and picked up a copy of Dr. Constantino's book, Engaging All Families. As I read it, a number of the points he made

resonated with me. It was rare to read of a secondary school that had tackled the issue of family engagement and had such positive results! The book has a section titled "A Comprehensive Evaluation for Family Engagement." I thought I would share my reading with my school council and suggest we form a working party to go through the process suggested by Dr. Constantino. Upon hearing of my plan, the school council agreed to my proposal.

Over the course of the next few months, the working party, which consisted of parents, students, school staff (both teaching and non–teaching), administrators, and community members, considered the questions posed in the evaluation process. We decided to run focus groups with families, students, and teachers. The working party meetings were some of the most insightful and meaningful I have ever attended in my career as an educator. I discovered that many of my assumptions about parental involvement were wrong. By listening, I learned what really concerned parents and found ways we could form meaningful partnerships.

One of the strong themes that emerged from the working party's discussions was the need for the school to develop a policy statement. The school needed to clarify how it saw the role of families and how the school would work with families.

In July 2006, we drafted a policy. We used the same framework of the process that we had used in the evaluation as a starting point for our policy document. So there were statements on a welcoming school culture, communication, assisting with home learning, valuing parent skills, encouraging parents to participate in school programs and decision–making processes, and using community resources to strengthen families.

After debate, discussion, and consultation across the Yea High School Community, the council ratified the final draft in November 2006.

At that same meeting, the school council also committed to forming a sub–committee called the

Partnership Action Team (PAT). Its makeup closely mirrors that of the original working party and it
is charged with working on the specifics of the policy statements. The school council desires action in
each of the areas identified in the policy. The PAT's
challenge is to identify strategies for each area and
ways they would be implemented within the school's
strategic plan.

We are still in the early days of our journey but
this process has awakened within the Yea High School
Community a desire to work in partnership with families and unlock "a force more powerful" in educating our
young people.

The Yea High School Family Engagement Policy is included below.

Yea High School Family Engagement Policy

Rationale

Yea High School is committed to working in
partnership with families. We believe that families
and the school, working as partners, will increase
student achievement and help students develop positive
attitudes.

Yea High School values the contribution of all
stakeholders, including teachers, parents, administrators,
the community, and the Department of Education
Victoria in developing partnerships that support student
outcomes.

Yea High School will continue to actively engage
with families and to identify new ways to develop and
strengthen school and family partnerships.

Policy Position

By engaging with families, we seek to:
* ensure that every aspect of the school culture is
open, helpful, and friendly
* help families understand what will support

their child's education and learning

- provide families with strategies and techniques that will assist their children with learning activities, and that will support and extend the school's program
- promote frequent two–way (school–to–home and home–to–school) communication about school programs and student progress
- provide opportunities for families to be involved in the school program
- value the skills and experiences that parents can contribute
- provide opportunities for family members to develop new skills
- encourage family members to actively participate in school decision–making and to develop skills in leadership, governance, and advocacy
- provide families with access to community and support services that strengthen school programs, family routines, and student learning and development

Things to Do:

1. *School boards and superintendents should review and revise a district school policy for family engagement.*
2. *Individual schools should use a family engagement correlate team of faculty, staff, and families, to either create or review and revise a sound family engagement policy.*
3. *Use the Yea High School process as a model to develop your school family engagement policy.*

53. A Vision for Families

Vision is an essential component of creating a positive school culture. As a well–known Proverb says, "Where there is no vision, the people perish." Organizations must possess a vision in order to provide forward momentum. In tandem with possessing a vision is the notion that someone, presumably the leader, must communicate that vision and convince stakeholders that the vision is worthy of their time, energy, and talent. But like so many other ideas in education, there seems to be great skepticism with regard to the importance of vision. Principals find themselves caught in a day–to–day quagmire and cannot even return phone calls, let alone ponder their vision for the school. Creating and communicating a vision for families helps all leaders remember an essential rule: focus on what is important, rather than what is urgent.

It serves all of us well to desire positive change and believe that all students can learn to their fullest capacity. We must put into place those systems and processes that will allow the space and flexibility to develop a vision for our school and to implement the programs, practices, procedures, and policies to move the school toward that vision. Investing in this concept is necessary to achieve the desired outcomes.

Almost all districts and schools have vision and mission statements. As stated in the last section, before trying to conceptualize a vision or mission statement, a district or school should concentrate on their statements of beliefs, or culture, which will guide the school and all of its people, attitudes, actions, policies, and decisions. Once a culture or belief statement is in place, both the district and member schools should capture a collective vision and mission to chart the course for success.

Both the vision (where are we going?) and the mission (how will we get there?) should be inclusive of the role of families. For example, if a vision incorporates the phrase "strong staff and programs," it could be adjusted to include families in this manner, "strong staff and family engagement and partnership supporting world–class programs."

Superintendent Steve Myers of the Toppenish School District in Toppenish, Washington expanded the vision and mission of his school district to include families. Originally, the district's signs, Web site, district letterhead, and other communication channels used the following phrase: "Where Students Come First and Teachers Make the Difference." After working within the Family Friendly Schools process, Mr. Myers and his team altered their statement to: "Where Students Come First and Teachers and Families Make the Difference."

Things to Do:

1. *With the input of students, staff, and families, revise the vision and mission of your school to be inclusive of family engagement as a core process.*
2. *Don't rush this experience. The process is as important as the statement crafted by the diverse team.*

54. Let Students Lead Family Conferences

Poor family attendance at parent–teacher conferences, especially at the secondary level, is a widespread challenge. Those families choosing not to attend the annual or bi–annual teacher–parent conference frustrate many educators. This is such a large problem that I began asking parents who did not attend conferences why they did not attend. There were certainly commonalities in the responses that I received.

Conference times during the workday were the barrier to participation cited most often. Many parents indicated that they couldn't leave work to attend a child's school conference. Parents who work in many areas of the service industry have little ability to attain the necessary time off to attend a school conference. Many parents fear losing their jobs if they request time off, and they may not receive payment for hours they do not work. Not having a paycheck outweighs the importance of attending the conference. For years, family engagement advocates have suggested alternative times for working parents such as evenings or weekends.

Many parents who have the opportunity and the means to attend the school conference still choose not to attend. When asked why, parents cite the lack of relevance. Many parents have the impression that teachers conduct conferences because of school or district requirements and that, given the option, would not conduct the conference. This impression stems from the numerous parents who report teacher absences at conferences. Further, many parents indicate that attending is not a good use of their time. They feel that they will hear information that they already know. When weighing decisions about time management, believing that a conference will produce no new insights into the success of a child weighs significantly in the decision whether or not to attend. One parent simply said to me, "If I go, all I am going to hear is the same thing I either heard before or already know. I never hear anything that I can use to help my child or any new information that can help me."

Considering the issue of conference scheduling and relevance to families, schools should adapt a flexible scheduling plan, but make the conferences mandatory. One strategy that works well is the idea of creating student–led or student–driven conferences. In this model, students become the centerpiece, not only sharing work and how they are doing in school, but making the conversation relevant to parents by explaining why they are doing the work they are doing and why they are achieving what they are. Elementary, middle, and high schools across the country implemented this model and used it in special education IEP (Individual Education Plan) meetings. Parent–family participation in conferences increases dramatically when students are involved in sharing and explaining their work and work habits.

Things to Do:

1. *Study the student–centered conference model. Research articles and books written on the subject and adapt the model to your school.*
2. *Work to create a flexible plan for conferences using evening and weekend hours.*
3. *Record the present level of conference attendance and track attendance with your new model to determine growth.*
4. *Survey parents and families as to what they would like to see added, deleted, or changed about parent conferences.*
5. *Set public goals for parent conference attendance (i.e., "this month's conference attendance percentage is ___"). Advertise your goals and progress toward goals much like a car dealer advertises sales toward the monthly goal.*

55. Make a Big LEAP for Parents and Families

Most schools create student handbooks. These handbooks share school policies and rules as well as services and programs available to students. Many schools now combine this information with a planner or agenda to promote student organization and achievement. It is an excellent idea to share this information with students in written format so that they can refer to it throughout the year. Unfortunately, many students, especially those in middle and high school, do not share the information with their families. As such, information that could be beneficial in building constructive relationships and improve the attitudes and behaviors of students as well as their academic achievement never gets to families.

Consider creating a "Parent/Family Handbook." At Stonewall Jackson, we found that many parents were asking the same questions so we began to create a list of "frequently asked questions." This evolved into our LEAP (Linking Education and Parents) program, a full–scale program that featured a handbook of information designed for parents. Furthermore, through surveys and telephone calls we found out what parents wanted to learn about school and held LEAP classes and workshops for parents.

Creating a handbook designed for parents and families helps to create a climate of trust and understanding as well as provide resources for continuous improvement. Other schools have added information for parents and families that help them assist children with homework and concepts being taught in school. The list of possibilities for a handbook is endless. Often, local community businesses and agencies will help defray the cost of the handbook because it is a way to support parents who are also employees. A parent/family handbook can be the start of a wonderful business partnership!

Things to Do:

1. *Collect thoughts from families about what information is helpful and relevant to them.*
2. *Determine information internally that will be helpful to families.*
3. *Create a parent/family handbook.*
4. *Work with local business partnerships or businesses to support and underwrite the project.*

5. *Print the book in multiple languages.*
6. *Request feedback in the form of surveys from parents each year to continue to revise and improve the handbook.*

56. Kickin' Child Care up a Notch

Kim Bauerle, a family engagement coordinator for the Anaheim Union High School District, suggests this new twist on a tested idea.

When asking caregivers to attend school meetings, workshops, activities, or functions, providing transportation and childcare are essential component in the equation to increase family attendance. In addition to childcare, advertise to parents that children can bring their homework or study materials and tutors will be on hand to assist children with work while parents and families attend the school function.

Work with your local high school National Honor Society, Beta Club, Future Teachers of America, or Student Council to attain high school students as tutors. Many high school students are looking for community service hours and a way to give back to the community. This vehicle provides the perfect opportunity. Schools that implement this program see a significant jump in family participation with school programs and functions.

Things to Do:

1. *Work with your local high school to attain high school students as tutors.*

2. *When scheduling evening or weekend meetings for parents and families, advertise tutoring and homework help in addition to childcare.*

3. *Record the families who attend. Thank them for the effort and interest.*

4. *Record the children who attend, their school, and class. Notify other principals of the child's efforts to acquire help with homework and tutoring. Watch the program grow.*

57. "Holy Toledo"

A few years ago, teachers and administrators at a local elementary school in Toledo, Ohio wanted to do something different to demonstrate their desire for strong family partnerships. With the blessing of the principal and staff development personnel, the teachers used a portion of their staff development day, on the day before the start of the school year, to make signs and travel though the neighborhoods that were served by their school. They were communicating a very simple message: We love you and can't wait to see you!

As the teachers traversed neighborhoods, more and more parents and students filled the streets, engaging them in conversation, trying to determine who their teacher would be, and getting answers to simple questions. The teachers arrived back to the school energized and the opening day was the very best the school had ever experienced.

Things to Do:

1. *Dedicate a day or a portion of a day prior to the school year to getting out into neighborhoods and welcoming families to the school.*
2. *Make some signs, bring some information, and have some fun! Make families feel welcome starting on the first day of school.*

58. A Few People All of the Time or All the People Some of the Time?

Dr. Larry Rowedder, a former superintendent in several school districts around the country, believed that getting continuous input from families provided better information than an annual survey.

He says, "Back in those days, we didn't have e–mail, so I sent out ten or so letters per week asking parents a few questions about our schools, principals, education, or issues that may have come up during the year. I invited parents to write me back, call me, or better yet, come by and visit with me in person. I found this system of collecting data extremely effective and in a year's time, I had acquired a healthy sample of the population."

Dr. Rowedder's idea can now be enhanced by telephone and internet survey tools, voice mail, e–mail, and even chat rooms and instant messaging. Schools can advertise electronic town meetings or invite parents to log onto Web sites to participate in a real–time discussion. Many schools are urging teachers to begin blogs (web logs) to help create dialogues using technology.

Things to Do:

1. *Determine a way to find a few questions (less than six) and invite a small group of people each week to respond.*
2. *Choose the medium that best suits your community. Even with rise in popularity of the Internet, a significant percentage of families are still not connected.*
3. *Keep a running total of responses and use the collected data to improve parent involvement efforts in your school.*
4. *Measure the perceptions of families that visit your school.*

59. Support the Middle

To help disengaged and disenfranchised families become involved, it is important to connect their needs to the needs of their children and the process of learning. Many children are doing an adequate job in school, but with additional support, could be doing superior work. These "children–in–the–middle" and their parents should not be neglected in your efforts to engage all families. With a little more encouragement from home and a little higher expectation from schools and classrooms, we can move many students from the middle to the top.

One of the ways to do this is by creating focus groups of 'children–in–the–middle." Determine what topics interest them and ask them if they think other parents would view these potential topics the same way. The next step is to take the information from the focus groups and develop a survey for all parents. Have them rate the topics they are interested in learning more about, and give them the opportunity to suggest additional topics. A strong commitment to this project will bring back a high rate of survey return. Middle schools and high schools might think about targeting incoming sixth and ninth grade parents as a way to begin this project.

Analyze the survey results and build a parent and family learning program around the most popular topics. Do not worry initially if you cannot connect the workshop to issues of specific student achievement. Meeting parent and family needs first will bring about a better opportunity for infusing more achievement–oriented programs later. At the conclusion of every program, relate what parents have learned to how they can support their child's learning at home. Make this a significant piece of every workshop you conduct.

Things to Do:

1. *Create a focus group of "families in the middle." Determine their needs and interests regarding their child's learning.*

2. *Create a survey based on the focus group feedback that invites all parents to share opinions and direction for family education programs.*

3. *Pick the top two or three programs that elicit the strongest support from families, publicize them, offer food, babysitting and tutoring for other youngsters, and transportation if necessary.*

4. *Measure and evaluate the success of the first program(s) that are completed. Build programs into the annual school plan from that point forward.*

60. When is a Barrier Not a Barrier?

The scenario is the same in almost every school. School administration and personnel plan a program that they feel is of interest to parents and families. They do every thing possible to encourage attendance. On the day of the big event, only a handful of parents and family members attend the meeting. Most of these families are the ones who regularly attend functions and are supportive of the school.

Administrators and teachers may assume that families are apathetic toward their children's learning. Nothing could be further from the truth. Chances are that one of the following barriers is keeping parents and families away:

1. *Timing*: The date, time, time of day, or day of the week is not conducive to the families for whom you are targeting the workshop.
2. *Parental uncertainty*: Many parents and families do not believe they are welcome in the school. Many were poor students or hold negative feelings about school. They want to be supportive, but their experiences do not allow them to attend.
3. *Culture:* Families for whom English is not a first language or families who are socio–economically disadvantaged are fearful of attending. The most significant reasons center on their feelings that school personnel have judged them in some way and any effort they make will not change the perception of educators at the school.
4. *Fear:* Families whose educational culture is such that the inferiority they feel morphs into a type of fear toward interacting with the school.

Research tells us that less than 2 percent of the parental population in the United States is truly apathetic toward their children's education. The remaining 98 percent find there are barriers like the ones highlighted above or others that prevent them from choosing to be actively involved.

Things to Do:

1. Believe that apathy is not the primary cause of disengagement.
2. Understand that low attendance means parent/family needs have not been met (timing, logistics, advertisement, or content).
3. Think strategically about the types of parent and family events that you have, and communicate these events in a manner that removes barriers.
4. When invited guests do not attend, find out what kept them from attending. Use this information to remove barriers to future attendance.

61. Outreach, Outreach, Outreach

There is a very simple rule to engage families who have traditionally been or have become disengaged: *before they will come to you, you must go to them.* If you have a school with five hundred students and your family meetings, seminars, and workshops are attracting less than thirty people, then families are not engaged. These families may feel uncertain about attending school functions.

As previously discussed, parental or family uncertainty is a huge issue, and it is one that is successfully addressed by Family Friendly Schools. Uncertainty occurs when families have negative experiences with school. These negative experiences are usually based on experiences their children have had with the school or experiences they had themselves while attending school. Uncertainty will also occur when families believe that they are being judged by their language, customs, or clothing, or when they feel ashamed or inadequate due to financial troubles. All of these issues are real and the most effective way to combat them is outreach.

School–related events that do not take place on the school property increase the likelihood that parents and family members will attend. For example, if you are having a meeting about upcoming testing, hold the meeting somewhere within the neighborhood. Middle schools and high schools can often use elementary facilities and see an immediate increase in the numbers of parents attending. However, moving meetings to another school location does not combat all of the forces working within uncertain parents.

Consider other places that are "neutral" and non–threatening to families. Throughout the years that we have been working with schools, we have generated quite a list of ideas: restaurants, supermarkets, laundromats, churches, synagogues, day–care facilities, libraries, local stores and businesses, parks, homeless shelters, and the list goes on and on. I often encourage educators to canvass their communities searching for the large numbers of places conducive to meetings for parents and families who, for whatever reason, are frightened or intimidated by the school environment. With a little thought, large lists of locations can be developed and used to promote real family engagement. Moving a meeting from a school to another location highlights the value you place in all parents and families and will go a long way toward re–culturing your school.

Things to Do:

1. *Understand the issues of uncertainty in parents and families. Help all staff become aware that changes in venues often produce more involvement and engagement.*
2. *Create a plan to determine spaces, places, and locations for important school meetings. (See my previous book "Engaging All Families" and the chapter on community asset mapping.)*
3. *Make a goal of moving a percentage of your events to locations within the community. Work toward moving half the meetings into neighborhoods and community areas that are less threatening to parents and families.*
4. *Record parent and family participation at outreach meetings. Develop goals and targets for family support and attendance at critical meetings.*
5. *Reward and thank parents for their attendance, contribution, and engagement.*

62. Action–Oriented Involvement in School Discipline

I vividly remember the first conversation I had with a principal who hired me as the new assistant principal. When discussing the difficulties of sharing negative disciplinary news with parents and families, he advised me to "sell the discipline." No parent or family member wants to hear about negative consequences such as detentions and suspensions. The principal informed me that many families displace the blame or challenge their child's discipline.

During my the first day on the job, a student got into a fight. I remembered everything that the principal told me. As soon as I said, "I am going to suspend your son," the mother took over the conversation. She said that the suspension from school was "giving him what he wants: a vacation." Few assistant principals have not heard this response toward suspensions from school. I needed an alterative to "sell the discipline."

Fortunately, the school leadership team already had another option to suspension in place. If parents and families were willing to accompany their child to a three–hour session during the evening or on Saturday, we would forgive the suspension in light of the family engagement with good school behavior. Our purpose was not to suspend but to keep a safe and orderly school environment. We determined that more effort in including parents and families in the solution would lower suspension rates and perhaps improve behavior. We were right on both counts. We were able to eliminate in–school suspensions altogether and our out–of–school suspension rate decreased by almost 40 percent. Teacher surveys indicated support for this method of dealing with discipline issues even though we were not suspending nearly as many students.

Our *Evening School at Stonewall* was a huge success. We incorporated counselors, local clergy, teachers, and other community support personnel to help us with the program. Poor school attitude and behavior is often a reflection of a child's life outside of school or a reflection of their family's attitude toward school. Bringing a team of people to work with the family not only helped to improve behavior in school, but gave many families the necessary support and resources to begin to take control of their home situations as well.

To further underscore the importance of action–oriented involvement in school discipline, here is one of my favorite stories about a parent, a tardy student, a little time, and my watch! A dad called me very upset that an assistant principal suspended his son for being tardy. He was convinced that the school was overcrowded and that his son was late because it was physically impossible to get to class. He demanded that I reverse the suspension immediately or he would be calling the superintendent, his board of education representative, and the local news channel!

Instead of getting into a heated debate, I invited the dad to come to school. He arrived at my office within twenty minutes, still angry with us. I assured him that if I could take a few minutes of his time, I could help him understand the issues at hand. I told him that if at the end of our time together he still felt that his son's discipline was inappropriate, I would remove it immediately. With that said, I began my plan.

I took off my wristwatch and handed it to Dad. I also gave him a map of the school identifying the class that his son left and the one to which he consistently arrived late. I gave Dad his son's locker number and combination as well as the location of all of the boys' restrooms that would be open during that time of day. I asked him to recreate his son's path several different ways, stopping in the restroom and at the locker. I told him he was free to wander around by himself. Dad took the map and the watch and set off on the trek. Classes were about ready to change, so he would have the full effect of our alleged "crowded hallways."

About fifteen minutes later, Dad reappeared at my door, only this time his demeanor was very different. He handed me my watch and apologized for his behavior on the telephone. He indicated that he walked, at a normal pace, stopped in the restroom and went to the locker. He took a few routes to the class and had at least two minutes to spare between each class. He said that there was no need to change the discipline. He also indicated that he would have a talk with his son and gave me his word that tardiness would no longer be an issue.

Most importantly, I said to him, "I know how tough it is to be a parent these days. I have a child at home myself. If you have a concern or a question, please feel free to stop by and visit any one the administrators or teachers. We welcome the time spent with parents to make new friends and help our kids." With that, we shook hands and Dad left. His son was never tardy to a class again.

Involving parents in disciplinary procedures can be more time consuming than the obligatory telephone call or mailed referral form.

The time spent up front in these situations ultimately saves time with repeated negative behaviors. When word gets out that parents are invited to come to school and walk to classes, students tend to move a little quicker!

Things to Do:

1. *Create a disciplinary review committee to develop programs and processes in which parents and families can be involved.*
2. *Determine frequency and types of disciplinary infractions that are occurring in your school. (This information is usually available in student management systems already in place.)*
3. *Consider several discipline programs that involve family input. Be sure parents know their due process rights for appeal.*
4. *One year after beginning the processes, collect discipline data again and compare with your baseline. Modify your program and plan accordingly.*

63. This is Me

I hear from parents around the country that each year they join school organizations and volunteer to be of assistance. Often, the school does not assign them a job. This frustration leads parents to disengagement with school activities.

Several years ago, I discovered an idea called "This is Me" by the "Original" Mike Smith of *Differencemakers, Ltd.* Parents who attended Back–to–School Night or Open House received a copy of the *This is Me* form, shaped like the outline of a person. They filled out pertinent contact information and listed their children and appropriate grade levels in school. On the left–hand side of the form were the words, "Things I like to do." On the right–hand side were the words, "Things I do not like to do." Family members filled in the forms with their own interests and strengths, as well as listing those activities or areas that were not of interest to them.

At the conclusion of the event, the forms were collected and the information entered into a database program. In one high school, the business education class created the database and entered the information as a class project.

At the first need for chaperones, the volunteer coordinator searched the database and located the names, addresses, e–mail addresses, and phone numbers of persons who indicated they liked to chaperone. When the drama department needed assistance with set building, those family members who indicated woodworking and painting interests were called on to assist.

Things to Do:

1. *Create a system for collecting and sorting family engagement information.*
2. *Contact parents when categories that match their interests and abilities are needed.*
3. *At least once during the school year, contact each person who completed the form and give them the opportunity to serve.*
4. *Collect pre– and post–data on parent volunteer rates and compare growth.*

64. Realtors Are Your Best Friends

I created the "Realtor Breakfast Program," to bring Realtors into our building and provide them with information about our school, our curriculum, our teachers, our successes, our philosophies, and our vision for a bright future. Each Realtor received packets of information to give to families considering the area. The packet included a personal invitation from me for any family to visit our school, anytime, with no appointment. I guaranteed that someone would always be available to give them a tour and answer their questions. I also invited the realtors to visit our school.

More than one hundred real estate professionals visited our school and witnessed firsthand the wonderful learning that was going on. I was amazed at how fast the information disseminated into the community. It took just days. Amazingly, parents and families who were already with us and not in the market for a house were also hearing the "buzz" about our school and we were seeing more people at functions, more hits on the Web site, and more families engaged in their children's education. The message was simple: *we need you.*

Things to Do:

1. *Call your local real estate organization and let them know your intentions. They will be happy to send you a listing of all of the realty companies and agents.*
2. *Mornings, before eleven o'clock., are good times for real estate workers. Usually by the noon hour, they are busy in model homes or working with clients. Breakfast seems to work the best.*
3. *Create packets of information that help engage families with their children and share pertinent information about the school.*
4. *Invite real estate professionals into your school for breakfast and an opportunity to walk the building to see the great things that are happening. End the session with the explanation and distribution of materials.*

65. Roll Out the Welcome Wagon . . . Right Into Their Living Room

As a gesture of true family engagement, develop "welcome wagons" that consist of staff and family liaisons to welcome new families through home visits. If strategically placed several days or weeks after the student enrolls at the school, such visits may serve to answer the questions that never came to mind during the new student registration.

Armed with a family address and gift basket, a home visit establishes a foundation for long–term trust, caring, and compassion in the home–school relationship.

Things to Do:

1. *Solicit staff members to serve on teams of three to four to make home visits.*
2. *Develop a standard welcome kit. Include the following types of items:*
   a. *A school brochure with demographic, academic, athletic, and extracurricular highlights*
   b. *General school contact information (school Web site, list of important phone numbers, and relevant staff members such as counselor or administrator)*
   c. *Parent or Family liaison contact information (person on "welcome wagon" team who would be willing to be available for follow–up questions)*
   d. *A gift. school sticker, shirt, or pen*
   e. *Community information generally available through local chamber of commerce: maps or local points of interest*
3. *Make an appointment with the family for a home visit instead of showing up unannounced.*
4. *Visit the family and watch relationships grow!*

66. State of the School Address

The "State of the School Address" provides an opportunity to celebrate accomplishments, update progress relative to school goals and priorities, and establish a course of future action. Each of these components is critical to the continuum of family engagement in schools. Knowledge leads to understanding and understanding leads to involvement, which are building blocks to engagement.

Compliment the principal's message and add further significance and value to the evening by inviting guest speakers. For example, at South Cobb High School, as the host of the "State of the School Address," the Parent Teacher Student Association (PTSA) sent invitational postcards in English and Spanish to all families. This format allowed further visibility to a growing PTSA and allowed for the PTSA Executive Board to take an active role in what was eventually perceived as a community "address" rather than exclusively a "principal's address." At the beginning of the meeting, the local school board representative and superintendent greeted the parents. Their participation added a dimension of district–wide support for the annual community forum.

Things to Do:

1. *Create an agenda for the evening. Invite guest speakers, such as the PTSA president, school board representative, and superintendent to make opening remarks prior to the principal's "State of the School Address."*
2. *Create informational packets for each guest.*
3. *Publicize the event through one or more of the following:*
   a. *Local television and print media*
   b. *Postcards to be mailed to each family (in native languages)*
   c. *School marquee*
   d. *School newsletter*
   e. *Automated phone system*
   f. *School Web site*

67. Connecting Families to School Improvement

Invite families to participate in School Improvement planning. Establish the expectation that families are included on all school committees, thereby seating teachers, administrators, and family members together during discussions of everything from academics to assessment, transportation to technology, and so on.

In addition to the practical value of including a family perspective in school improvement discussions, this process also creates a subtle opportunity to guide the school culture toward systemic family engagement. Just as educators talk about "teachable moments," consider the following "culture moments" that would be born through distributed, consensus–driven family engagement in school improvement:

1. *Faculty meetings:* Rather than offer the traditional "committee report" from the mouth of a teacher or administrator at the next faculty meeting, consider inviting a family member to discuss the progress on the school improvement goal relative to the use of formative assessments to guide instruction.

2. *Family forums:* Host similar sessions that are by families, for families. If families are genuinely engaged in the committee processes, they will be just as equipped and prepared to present information and respond to family questions. For example, family members on the school safety and security committee can host a parent forum at the local community center on behalf of the safety and security committee. During this meeting, they can present school data, committee minutes, short/long–term goals, and facilitate a question–and–answer session. Follow–up questions and general perceptions can then be shared with the committee, and even better, at the next faculty meeting!

Organizational Structure for School Improvement Plan

The model below represents the school improvement initiative at South Cobb High School to address the goals of distributed leadership, consensus building, and inclusion relative to the Georgia School Improvement Standards. (Note that school Performance

Standards listed below under "Standards Committees" are specific to the eight standards required by the state of Georgia for all public schools. Use your state education Web site to determine the appropriate standards.)

School Improvement Council
(SIP Governing Body)

Primary Functions:
- Create SIP
- Review policies, procedures, and practices
- Formulate budget (nexus between funds and SIP)
- School vision, mission, beliefs

▼

Standards Committees
(Includes the eight Georgia School Performance Standards, denoted with *)
+ Technology Committee + Communication Committee)

- Instruction *
- Curriculum *
- Assessment *
- Planning and Organization *
- Professional Learning *
- Student, Family, and Community *
- Leadership *
- Culture *
- Technology
- Communication

▼

Faculty, Students, Community
(Responsibility to inform all stakeholders of SIP goals, action steps, and benchmarks)

Stakeholder Representation

The School Improvement Council consists of the following members:

- Principal
- Assistant Administrator (two)
- Chair From Each Standards Team (ten)
- Family Members (three–five)
- Student Leaders (four)
- Business Leader (one)

The Standards Committee consist of the following members:

- Administrator(s)
- Department Chair(s)
- Elected Chair (Not Administrator or Department Chair)
- Teachers (Voluntary)
- Parents
- Students

Strategies for Successful Engagement of Families in the School Improvement Process

- *Family presentations:* Invite family members of each committee to present school improvement action plans, benchmarks, and progress reports at faculty meetings, PTSA meetings, and via e–mail to staff.
- *Family voice in school newsletter:* Establish regular family columns in the school newsletter or Web site that detail family engagement in the school improvement processes.
- *Give family members ownership of parts of the school improvement process:* Invite members of each committee to distribute and analyze family engagement surveys. Invite other parents and families to serve as members of the school improvement committees.

Things to Do:

1. Create a school improvement and oversight model that has a family engagement component to it.
2. Involve families on all school committees.
3. Use faculty meetings and family forums to highlight the work of families with regard to school improvement and governance.
4. Give families meaningful roles and responsibilities with regard to total school improvement.

68. The Staff Field Trip

I asked Dr. Grant Rivera, principal at South Cobb High School in Atlanta, Georgia about the benefits of knowing the families and homes of children. He wrote the following:

Perhaps the most powerful message I could send as a school principal is to knock on the door of a student in my care and sit in the family's living room to discuss their child's education. Adults always appreciate and respect the value of my time. The time I spend in a home, motivated only by the success of their child, can create goodwill in a relationship that often carries us through any difficult times that may lie ahead. In addition to the positive feelings created for the family, in the heart and mind of at least one principal, every home visit brings the realities and challenges that at least one student brings to school each day.

Sunnyside High School is in an agricultural district in the heart of Yakima Valley, Washington. The diverse student population of over fifteen hundred includes 82 percent Hispanic, 16 percent Caucasian, and 2 percent other. Approximately 85 percent of the student body qualifies for fee–reduced lunch. Ryan Maxwell is an assistant principal at Sunnyside High School and acts as the school improvement facilitator. Ryan shares how a faculty and staff "field trip" helped create a dialogue and better understanding between families and the school:

As part of our commitment to family engagement, we have worked hard to find strategies that will be successful. Three years ago, we brought Family Friendly Schools in to begin this process. They presented ideas to our entire staff about ways to engage parents, and we integrated many of the ideas into our school improvement plan. One idea, the bus trip, intrigued our staff, so we decided to try it.

We contacted Hispanic parents that had been involved in the past to help with this endeavor. These parents contacted other parents from areas around Sunnyside who would be willing to assist with the bus trip. The bus trip was set to take place during a week of training before school began. We separated our teachers onto two buses and had them start on opposite sides of town. We had the buses stop in five locations, which took about ten minutes each. When the bus stopped, a parent would come onto the bus and talk about what life was like in his/her neighborhood. The unexpected outcome of these stops was that parents also opened up about what they wanted out of Sunnyside High School. One mother became very emotional as she talked about her family's struggles and that her son wanted to join the wrestling team, but the family couldn't afford shoes. She didn't realize that our school had a fund that assisted with these types of issues. Conversations like this were the norm that day. Teachers realized that our students come from homes where parents want desperately for their children to succeed, but often resources stand in their way. A bridge was created that day thanks to the bus trip.

Consider such a field trip for your school staff. The goal is to expose staff to the range of socio–economic conditions and dynamics that make up your school community. Reaching out in this manner will produce several outcomes: 1) greater appreciation and awareness of the community for staff members; 2) relieve fear of the unknown that may keep staff members from feeling comfortable and confident enough to make the home visit; and 3) provide understanding to spark conversation and common ground between staff members and families.

Things to Do:

1. *Secure a school bus during school–year planning days.*
2. *Obtain a tour guide who can provide relevant information about the community. Consider a family member, alumnus, school board member, or local government representative.*
3. *Plan a thirty to forty minute tour that covers the range of socio– economic conditions and community points of interest.*
4. *For an added touch, stop at a local ice cream shop at the close of your tour so the local high school students can serve the staff!*

69. Celebrate Culture

At South Cobb High School, with the guidance of a staff member, Hispanic/Latino students formed *Voz Latino*, a student–led group designed to inform and promote social, political, and educational issues relevant to the Hispanic/Latino community. While the explicit goal was to educate Hispanic/Latino students and families as well as the larger school population, the group also served as a social bridge within and between cultures to promote family engagement in schools. For example, each semester, *Voz Latino* hosts a family night. The club members personally invite Hispanic/Latino families to bring a covered dish to the school. During this time, teachers and students facilitate conversations between families throughout dinner.

The goal of the evening is three–fold. First, given the intrinsic desire by many families to share culture–specific food and experiences with others, the covered dish social serves as a unique invitation for students and their extended families to come into the school building and share their culture. Second, families have opportunities to network with other families who share similar cultural backgrounds and native languages. Third, to compliment the cultural significance of the evening, teachers and students can present information to families that promotes engagement in school. Examples of educational resources offered during the *Voz Latino* social include the following:

1. Family handbook and calendar of events (Spanish version)
2. Community resources
3. Language–specific points of contact at school
4. Syllabi and course materials (Spanish version)

Things to Do:

1. *Identify a group of students and/or teachers with an interest in cultural issues, such as the Cultural Diversity Club, and/or a student–specific group, such as Voz Latino, which represented the school's Hispanic/Latino students and families.*
2. *Designate an evening and invite families to bring a covered, native dish.*
3. *In an effort to improve attendance, be mindful of the cultural tendencies regarding time of day and day of the week. In addition,*

encourage students to follow up with interested families by phone (in native language) during the week of the event.

4. *Develop an agenda for the evening. Include time for sharing stories, recipes, and other culturally significant events (such as salient political or social issues).*

5. *Identify specific family engagement outcomes that may include one of the following goals:*

   a. *Each family has a familiar point of contact in the building for future communication needs.*

   b. *Each family receives a course syllabus in their native language.*

   c. *Each family receives the contact information for another school family who has a child similar in age, interest, etc.*

70. Know your Families' Businesses!

In every town and city, there are businesses that employ large numbers of adults from that particular community. Furthermore, within the same communities, there are local establishments popular with students and their families.

Enhance family engagement by building strong relationships with these respective businesses. Given the natural ties that families have with businesses as an employee or customer, such locations serve as easy targets for mutually beneficial relationships. Consider the following examples of school–family–business partnerships:

1. Invite the business to serve as a formal Partner in Education.
2. Include the business in the regular school e–mail blasts and request this information be forwarded to all business employees.
3. During school recognition events, have the business join the staff during presentation of awards. For formal events, invite the business to be a formal presenter for the "attendance award." For more informal events, such as providing an ice cream sandwich to all students following final exams, invite the employees to assist in handing out food to students.
4. For assistance with day–to–day operations, request that the local business support school volunteer opportunities. For example, Wal–Mart employees were invited to volunteer in the school cafeteria. On "Wal–Mart Days at South Cobb High School," the employees wear their Wal–Mart uniform and assist with clean up and supervision during their lunch break or day off.
5. Offer student volunteer organizations and student performance groups like the chorus or band to assist with special events at the business such as a grand opening or holiday party.
6. Donate historic pictures, school crests, and memorabilia for the business to post in visible locations.

Things to Do:

1. *Identify those businesses that are prominent employers of school families and/or are popular with students and families.*
2. *Offer mutually beneficial opportunities: use the varied personnel and material resources within the school to determine if businesses are "getting" as much as they are "giving."*
3. *Create opportunities for regular two–way interaction that extends beyond the front doors of the establishment to involve the families impacted by the particular business.*

71. Engaging Forums

Schools can share information with the community through district–wide forums. A successful forum requires time, energy, and preparation. Unfortunately, because of that investment, schools and districts usually stop with one forum. In order to cultivate a following, a series of well–publicized and executed forums are needed. When this occurs, families recognize them as a continuing and familiar process.

We know that when programs and workshops are meaningful and relevant to families, more people will attend and, in turn, benefit from the information shared. In the North Penn School District (NPSD), Family Engagement Coordinator Linda Abram shares the following story about how such a forum series has become very popular in the community.

In early 2004, NPSD Superintendent Dr. Bob Hassler sought to establish and strengthen relationships that would promote and enhance student achievement, as well as engage the community in a discussion about relevant educational topics. As superintendent of schools, Dr. Hassler serves a school district comprised of eighteen schools, over thirteen thousand students, eight municipalities, and ninety thousand residents in the suburbs of Philadelphia, Pennsylvania.

To join Dr. Hassler in this ambitious endeavor, he invited individuals from public and private schools, faith–based organizations, health and human service agencies, local colleges, civic organizations, and the media, plus local business professionals, educators, students, and parents, including those who home school their children. From this initial meeting, he formed the North Penn Community Forum Committee, which examined the concept of offering a series of informative educational forums, seminars, and discussions serving the greater community and addressing current educational and social issues. Desired outcomes included developing open lines of communication to enable collaboration, creating a shared vision within the North Penn community, engaging families in thought provoking and informative sessions, providing opportunities for learning about how model schools address the needs of students, and providing learning opportunities for educators to experience the latest thinking in their profession.

More than twenty committee members joined Dr. Hassler in a series of meetings designed to help the members learn how to function as a team and how to brainstorm and build a consensus, which ultimately positioned them for forum planning and development. Through an overview process, the committee mapped out a full range of actions necessary to accomplish the goal of planning and executing all aspects of successful forums. A steering committee and subcommittees accomplished all of these tasks. A schedule of meetings was established. Topics were chosen through committee input, surveys, and community needs. A media campaign and community networking supported each forum.

In addition to my presentations, the Community Forum has hosted renowned speakers such as Dr. Willard Daggett (*Making Good Schools Great*) and Dr. Michele Borba (*Raising Good Kids* and *Strengthening Your Child's Social Skills: Addressing Issues Youth Face Today*). Community Forums in workshop format have also been held featuring presenters who addressed topics such as Internet safety, adolescence, and bullying. All of the Community Forums provided families, educators, and community members with opportunities for learning as well as time to ask questions of these experts in their fields.

Free babysitting is always available for school–aged children during the forums. In addition, light refreshments and an expo of awareness tables provide information on services and programs in the community and in the school district. High school students volunteer to assist with a variety of tasks including greeting participants, distributing programs, collecting surveys, assisting in setup, and providing directional assistance. Committee members and various volunteers assist at each forum in a variety of ways. Professional development credit is offered for both preschool teachers as well as certified educators. Support staff members often receive incentives to attend as well.

The program continues to grow and expand as feedback from surveys collected at each forum is used to plan future events. Feedback from participants was very positive, including:

- "Great job, topics have been very relevant and informative."
- "I believe it is important that the Forum continues to address these issues."
- "Extremely enlightening! The presentation really opened my eyes."

- "Good chance to network with other parents as well as a good source of information."
- "I would recommend the Forums because as times change, you need to be educated about new and upcoming issues to stay on top of things."
- "Powerful and necessary messages."
- "Excellent topics for deeper thought and reflections."
- "Excellent way to involve all community members."
- "Topics are relevant to every day parenting"
- "The Forums can help us work together as a community in tackling and addressing important issues."
- "Because family involvement is of utmost importance for student success, people need to hear this over and over."

Over two thousand people attended the forums in the first three years since the series' inception. The composition of the North Penn Community Forum committee has grown and changed to reflect the needs and interests of the community. The momentum created will only increase as NPSD further engages all stakeholders in lifelong learning and ensuring achievement for all students.

Things to Do:

1. *Create a steering committee for your community forum series.*
2. *Survey your families and community members regarding topics of interest.*
3. *Set explicit goals and outcomes for your events. Provide evaluations and feedback forms at every event.*
4. *Follow the North Penn plan of childcare, light refreshments, high–profile speakers, and an information expo.*
5. *Collect names and track attendance at the events to help continue and grow your forum program.*

72. Develop a *Real* Compact for Learning

Every Title I school is required to have a "Compact for Learning," which is a commitment to sharing responsibility for student learning and an action plan for a family–school–community partnership to help children get a high–quality education. Teams of educators and families create the compacts. These documents clarify what families and schools can do to help children reach high standards. Even though it is a requirement, writing a compact is a wonderful idea for any school serious about promoting real family engagement.

In part, federal legislation indicates the following regarding learning compacts:

> . . . each school served under this part shall jointly develop with parents for all children served under this part a school–parent compact that outlines how parents, the entire school staff, and students will share the responsibility for improved student achievement and the means by which the school and parents will build and develop a partnership to help children achievement the State's high standards.

Such a compact shall:

1. Describe the school's responsibility to provide high–quality curriculum and instruction in a supportive and effective learning environment that enables the children served under this part to meet the State's student performance standards; the ways in which each parent will be responsible for supporting their children's learning, such as monitoring attendance, homework completion, and television watching; volunteering in their child's classroom; and participating, as appropriate, in decision relating to the education of their children and positive use of extracurricular time; and
2. Address the importance of communication between teachers and parents on an ongoing basis through, at a minimum:
   a. parent–teacher conferences in elementary school, at least annually, during which the compact shall be discussed as the compact relates to the individual child's achievement;

b.   frequent reports to parents on their children's progress; and
c.   reasonable access to staff, opportunities to volunteer and
     participate in their child's class, and observation of classroom
     activities.

Things to Do:

1.   *Form a committee of family members and educators together to
     create a compact.*
2.   *Review and revise the compact annually.*

73. Create a Project and Testing Calendar

My wife, Peggie, was the International Baccalaureate Program Coordinator at Garfield High School in Woodbridge, Virginia. As the program at Garfield grew, so did the problems with assignment and examination conflicts and overloads. To solve the problem, Peggie instituted a project and testing calendar. Every teacher was required to post major projects and tests on one uniform calendar. Every teacher had access to view the calendar and immediately knew when it was or was not appropriate to assign major projects or tests. Peggie worked with families to help them understand the calendar and worked with their children on issues of stress and time management.

Helping parents and families understand expectations for their children promotes home discussion and support for learning. Any grade level, department, or team can incorporate the calendar concept to support students and families in the quest for high achievement.

Things to Do:

1. *Check to see if your school software includes a group calendar option.*
2. *Work with teachers to agree on a process to create and update the calendar.*
3. *Inform families of the calendar and allow them access. For those families that do not have access to the internet, allow them the opportunity to hear messages by phone, or supply hard–copies of the calendar on a weekly or bi–monthly basis.*

74. Rides for Conferences

An easily solved barrier to attendance at school conferences is lack of transportation.

Contact your local taxi company, bus line, or train line and ask if they would partner with the school by offering either free or reduced fares for families who need transportation to school conferences. In places where this has been implemented, most transportation agencies were skeptical about this plan, but then saw the community and publicity benefits for their business.

Here is how this idea works. First, let the transportation organizations know that you will publicize their efforts and make them an official partner of the school. Reward them with a plaque that they can display, demonstrating their support for the local school. Create an official voucher for transportation. The voucher is dated and good for a "one time only" ride. Some transportation agencies have provided schools their own free coupons or, in some cases, bags of subway tokens that can be given to parents and family members who attend conferences. Either way, your school and community partners can work together to promote more family engagement in student conferences at school.

Things to Do:

1. *Schedule a meeting with each of your local transportation agencies and companies. Convince them (with your charm and sales ability!) that you need them to participate in a program that will ultimately benefit children.*

2. *Provide free or reduced fare transportation to and from the conferences. Create a process that is easy for both parent and professional, whether it is a letter, card, coupon, or token.*

3. *Publicize and recognize transportation agencies that will assist you as partners in education. Have a ceremony to honor their help, take pictures, and send to all local media outlets. Give the company a plaque or gift to display in their offices.*

4. *If the transportation companies and agencies cannot do it alone, solicit help from local businesses to offset costs of free or reduced fare coupons for transportation.*

75. Technology that Teaches Engagement

Almost every school has an informative and colorful Web site. Why not take it a step further and link your site to student learning? In addition to all of the useful announcements, calendars, lunch menus, and communication that presently exist, put links to downloadable documents that will help families support learning at home.

Student achievement data will determine which learning areas to target on the site. For example, if your sixth grade students have specific weaknesses with the math strands, then create information sheets, games, or worksheets that concentrate on that area.

Collect data including site–guest's name, and the name and grade of his or her child This information will provide data about frequency of use and about individual site guests, which helps determine if your ideas and energy are producing the desired results.

Things to Do:

1. *Create a learning link on your school Web site home page.*
2. *Using student achievement data, formulate information that can be downloaded or accessed by parents and families to understand what is being taught, but to also help their children and support learning at home.*
3. *Include practice questions and problems on the Web site.*
4. *Require login information to measure use of the information you are creating and sharing. Adjust your efforts if the results are not meeting your expectations.*
5. *Publicize the learning features of your home page to all parents using their spoken language through all communication channels.*

76. Real Parent–Teacher Groups

There is an old saying that rings true: *People do not care how much you know until they know you care.* Building relationships with parents and families who participate in different groups and organizations is an important step in laying the foundation for successful family engagement.

Principals and teachers should participate in a few parent–led activities. One of the biggest criticisms of many parent–teacher organizations is that few, if any, teachers join or participate in the organization. Principals should look at expectations of teachers and rearrange or revise duties so that there can be some involvement in parent organizations.

Often, the only time administrators and teachers participate in parent–led activities is when parent support, usually financial, is needed. This can undermine relationships very quickly. Consider rotating a teacher and administrator through the organizations to represent the school at each meeting and event. Parents and families understand that principals and teachers have lives too, and they do not expect the principal or a group of teachers to attend every function. However, the effort to have representation at the organizational meetings will go a long way in sending the message that school employees value parents and believe their participation is critical in the life of a child.

Things to Do:

1. *Create a process that allows for teacher/administrative representation at all parent–led meetings and activities.*
2. *Ensure that the families know the representative is a direct conduit to the teaching staff or principal.*
3. *Create a process for communicating parent information to the entire staff within twenty–four hours of the meeting or activity.*

DOMAIN

4

SCHOOL SUPPORT FOR HOME LEARNING

77. Front and Center with Families

Parent/family centers go a long way to help build relationships with all families. Parent centers are a marvelous way to reach out to migrant families, limited or non–English speaking families, disadvantaged families, foster families, minority families, homeless or sheltered families, and others who are traditionally disenfranchised from the school and its environment.

Parent/family resource centers provide an outreach opportunity to help families learn and understand important concepts such as due process, communicating with school or district personnel, and navigating the special education system. The centers also provide training opportunities to help families become more confident in their parenting skills and their ability to support home learning, as well as learn English or another language.

Moving beyond the traditional parent centers, many have now included classes for families so that they may learn for the first time or have a refresher class in the same subjects that their children are learning in school. This is an extremely effective way to help families create home learning environments and increase their efficacy in helping their children academically.

The Boston Public School System created a pilot program of Family and Community Outreach Coordinators in seventeen Boston public schools at the elementary, middle, and high school levels. Most of the schools served by these outreach positions have created parent/family resource centers within the school. Family

Friendly Schools conducted an evaluation of the program in early 2006. According to interviews, focus groups, and surveys, parents and families overwhelmingly appreciated the family centers. Classes, information, mediation, conflict resolution, translation, and general information are all made available to parents who have traditionally been disassociated with the school. In many schools, the outreach coordinator is conducting classes in math, English, and reading so that parents can learn as their children do and understand how they can support learning at home. Families and parents who are reluctant or intimidated by the school, its environment, and its staff, gravitate to the family center as a first stop along the way to building a better relationship with their child's school.[7]

Things to Do:

1. *Create a space within your school for a family center.*
2. *Have furniture and room items donated by local organizations to make the room look like a home.*
3. *Create informational items that parents can take and share.*
4. *Appoint a family center coordinator, part–time if necessary, to work directly with families in the community.*
5. *Schedule classes and information sessions in the family centers for family members.*

---

7   Constantino, S.M. (2003) *Engaging All Families: Putting Research into Practice.* Scarecrow Press: Lanham, MD.

78. Engage Families with Professional Development

I often tell a story of the parent who seems to be perpetually angry with her child's school, and I name her "Mrs. McNasty." Mrs. McNasty is a parent who finds something wrong with everything the school tries to do and takes every opportunity to voice her negativity all over the school and community. School personnel usually react negatively to Mrs. McNasty. The more the school tries to isolate her, the worse her attitude and complaints against the school and its staff become. Even though Mrs. McNasty is a fictitious character, many educators can relate to the characterization, and it does not take them very long to conjure up in their minds a real parent who fits the description of a Mrs. McNasty.

Anger is a mask for fear. It makes sense that if we can give Mrs. McNasty the tools to be engaged in her child's education, she might not be quite as "McNasty" as she is. The best way to accomplish this task is to promote staff development sessions to all families. Let them know that teachers will be learning new teaching strategies. Invite them to be a part of the training, so they might learn right along with teachers. The dividends are twofold. First, parents get an idea of what is taught and can apply that to their own children. Second, parents and teachers are able to form a relationship, build trust, and communicate, thus alleviating the barrier of fear that so often interrupts the ability of teachers and families to have real relationships.

Here is a true story of a Mrs. McNasty, who was invited to a staff development session on learning styles. This particular parent had had a run-in with just about every teacher, counselor, principal, and coach in the school. The teachers at the program were petrified when they saw her walk in. They were sure her only purpose was to disrupt, agitate, and complain.

The workshop started and teachers and parents together began to understand the concepts and how they might be applied in classroom situations with specific groups of students. A particularly brave teacher began a dialog with Mrs. McNasty. Toward the end of the session, the moderator noted that Mrs. McNasty and the teacher sitting next to her were crying. Fearing the worst, the moderator approached the two women and found that just beneath the surface of the table they were holding hands. When the moderator inquired about the problem, Mrs. McNasty said through her tears, "I never knew that she wanted me involved," to which the teacher added, "I never knew she wanted to *be* involved." From that day forward, Mrs. McNasty shed her angry persona and became a staunch school supporter.

Things to Do:

1. *Identify staff development sessions that families could attend and from which they could garner information.*
2. *Publicize staff development and personally invite families to participate.*
3. *Underscore the notion that a family member is a child's first and best teacher.*

79. Explain Expectations to Families for Increased Home Engagement

Research clearly identifies that all families, regardless of the culture or income, see education as a key to future happiness and success for their children. Often, however, these families do not understand the state and local standards for student achievement.

Every school district should create a public relations program that helps all families understand local and state expectations. Often, the "Frequently Asked Questions" format is effective to put questions and answers into language that all parents and families can understand. The translation of these documents also begins to help those families for whom English is not a first language. Printing information and disseminating it among families, however, is not enough. Writing is only one form of communication, and there is no way to know if the recipient has read or understood the communication.

A public relations professional once told me that if you want somebody to acknowledge and remember something, you must provide the information in five different ways. In addition to writing information, communicating the information face–to–face is extremely beneficial as it gives instant feedback. Using the local media (newspapers, local publications, and local interviews) is also a good way to communicate information. Community forums in locations other than the school are beneficial for those families unable or unwilling to come to the school. The use of flyers, church bulletins, advertisements, Web sites, and e–mail all help to share important information and educate parents and families on school expectations of their children.

A shopping center or mall is also a unique way to share information. Contact the local manager and ask if you can set up a table or kiosk over the course of several weekends. Staff the station with volunteers who are knowledgeable about the school's expectations. This also works in other public venues. When a family stops by, record their name and their child's name

Use your student management software to determine which parents are receiving the message and which are not. This type of measurement will help focus on strategies for those parents and families who are not getting the important messages about school expectations. Often the only way to reach those families is have school staff or knowledgeable volunteers visit the home and share the information.

Do not be afraid to ask the following questions: 1) Do you understand the information that I am sharing with you? 2) Can you think of any questions that you might have about the information? 3) Can I count on you to support your child's learning at home through (suggest a strategy or strategies)? 4) What is the best time and manner to contact you in the future?

Asking these questions sends a clear message that we care enough about children's learning and the important role that parents play to create a platform for continuous communication.

Things to Do:

1. *Create a five–layered public relations plan to share local and state expectations of children.*
2. *Train volunteers to assist you in sharing information with families.*
3. *Talk to local businesses where many families spend their time. Determine a way to communicate to families through these businesses.*
4. *Document the names of people that received and understood the information.*
5. *Use home visits and other face–to–face meetings to share the information and help all parents and families understand expectations.*
6. *Ask the "closing questions." Determine the best manner in which to contact a parent and family, and then use that process to build a relationship with them.*

80. Build Home Support for School Rules, Regulations, and Procedures

School safety continues to be a major focus of schools and a major concern for families. Parents and families want to know that the school is a safe place for learning. Student rules and regulations are critical to school safety. Building level rules must comply with district or state codes that outline expected behaviors and consequences for violations of those behaviors. Principals often lament that families are supportive of rules and regulations until their children become involved in a problem.

What we know to be true with students works equally well with families. When formulating rules for which there is local control (i.e. tardiness, dress, etc.), work to involve parents, families, and community in the decision–making process. The larger the role families can play in helping to create rules and regulations, the more likely they will support them when an infraction occurs.

Ask for input from parents at meetings. Use the telephone to survey parents about rules and regulations. (Some telephone systems have built in survey devices that make this very easy.) Post a web survey that allows both students and parents to register their opinions. Request input through your newsletters or a separate mailing. If you are at a secondary school, allow student groups the time to review the codes and provide their input into rules and regulations.

The majority of people understand the need for rules and will be reasonable in their input. Undoubtedly, there will be one or two who offer inappropriate suggestions. Do not let this small group keep you from involving parents in rule making.

Educators must realize that they do not possess all of the answers and are not always correct. Accept the fact that no one person or group of persons has a monopoly on good ideas or intelligence. Work with all parents and families to determine the best course of action. Keep in mind that changing a rule based on the suggestion of parents or students is not the end of the world. In many cases, a rule works well largely because of the buy–in of families and students.

Things to Do:

1. *Create a plan that allows parents, families, and students to discuss and offer input and suggestions on school rules and regulations.*
2. *Invite collaboration on these issues. Collaboration results in an improved product.*
3. *Create a draft of the rules and regulations for the following year during the present school year. Make the document available, and seek feedback prior to its adoption by the school council.*
4. *Educate families about the rules that are mandated by the school board or by state law and the consequences that could follow breaking them. Make sure parents understand that some disciplinary infractions will cause automatic suspension, or worse, recommendations for expulsion.*

81. A Focus on Disengaged Families

Support for home learning is a significant pathway to improved student achievement. Families lacking the educational capital to support their children are isolated from their children's learning and achievement. Some think that families who are not educated themselves can offer little in support of their children. If that were the case, our society would never evolve.

Most schools offer evening meetings and workshops for families on a variety of subjects. Unfortunately, the families who really need to attend these affairs are usually absent. In a few investigations of such programs, we found that the parents who were attending all had children who were receiving high grades and meeting with great success in school. In order to involve disengaged families, more planning and focused implementation must be done in order to maximize the benefit.

Start by understanding that not all families may need to be engaged—some already are. Identify those students who, at a particular grade level or for a particular subject, are achieving at levels that do not meet school expectations. Look for patterns and trends among these students. What characteristics, if any, do all or most of these students have in common? Once patterns can be determined, highlight the parents and families of these students. Ask other families to join the process through invitations, phone calls, and home visits. Create sessions designed to help them navigate the school system and help their children. Offer transportation and childcare to help parents and families attend.

South Cobb High School has successfully implemented a program for families of students who are not meeting required standards, as part of the overall school improvement plan. For example, in one small group, nine of ten special education students who had previously failed end–of–course tests passed them successfully after one year in the program. Today, South Cobb High School has the highest percentage of special education students graduating with a regular education diploma in the state of Georgia.

Kim Bauerle, FFS trainer and Family Involvement Coordinator for the Anaheim Union High School District in Anaheim, California, has instituted an "Academic Boot Camp" for parents and families. Dressed in fatigues and shouting commands like a drill sergeant,

Bauerle brings in hundreds of limited or non–English speaking families, minority families, and socio–economically disadvantaged families to the Boot Camp. This program helps families understand standards and expectations for their children and gives them practical, hands–on suggestions for helping their children become successful.

Teachers at Carver Elementary School in Wayne County, North Carolina, offered families an opportunity to partner for their children's success. It was a great way to start the school year off by engaging families in grade–level parent/teacher sessions designed with interactive hands–on activities to help parents at home. Carver teachers recognized that families are a child's first teacher and looked forward to the parent/teacher sessions to share and model for families some of their successful techniques used in the classroom. The techniques shown by classroom teachers helped give families more resources to use during the school year at home. The sessions provided an opportunity for families to practice strategies in a non–judgmental environment and encouraged parents to network with each other in sharing information and problem solving. The teachers were excited in knowing that these techniques, when transferred from the classroom to the home, would help parents reinforce skills the teachers were using to prepare the children for success in the classroom, the Kindergarten through Second Grade Literacy Assessments, and the End–of–Grade Tests. Dinner was provided for families, along with materials to use at home and a certificate of attendance. Children were motivated to bring their families for a "special night out" as they received homework assistance along with special activities designed for these sessions. The following month, family participation was celebrated with a "Family Reading Night," that included a guest author.

Things to Do:

1. *Determine students who are falling below minimum standards in particular subjects or grade levels.*
2. *Design parent involvement training programs that can help families support their children in an effort to raise achievement.*
3. *Record baseline data prior to the effort and then again at the conclusion. Note strengths and weaknesses, and make corrections as necessary.*

4. *Compare testing successes from before the programs through one, two, and three years of the program. Longitudinal data should steadily rise.*

82. Start a Family Book Club

A major focus of school improvement continues to be reading improvement. Lack of reading skill continues to be a prime culprit in low student performance. To increase the likelihood of students' reading on grade level, incorporate strategies that involve families in reading improvement initiatives.

Family literacy is an effective strategy when working with students to attain appropriate levels of reading. Family literacy also promotes the important aspect of supporting learning at home. Many schools, however, stop at the simple notion of telling families that it is important for them to read with their children. In many families, especially those for whom English is not a first language and those that are socio–economically disadvantaged, schools should take an additional step in promoting reading by creating different types of book clubs for parents.

The Family Literacy Backpack Program, sponsored by the Buddy Project (www.buddyproject.org), is an idea to get your creative juices flowing. This project gives you systematic instructions for obtaining and filling backpacks with books to loan to families. Different months center on different themes. The Buddy Project is one of dozens of ideas and projects out there to promote family literacy.

A Family Book Club is another great idea to promote family reading. The book could be one that is being read in school or a fun book that will capture the imagination of children. Keep abreast of family reading and discussion about the book through good two–way communication. Create a calendar that is easy for families to follow and will help them keep up with their reading and discussion. Provide discussion questions and ideas to promote learning at home. At the conclusion of the semester or year, have a book club party and display a list of books read and the names of families participating.

Promoting literacy to families promotes literacy among students. One of the best resources for families and school staff is *Taking the Guesswork Out of School Success*[8] by Dr. Joni Samples. Dr. Samples provides great information to families and school staff on standards, testing, and other issues that are important for parents to understand.

---

8   Samples, J. (2003). *Taking the Guesswork Out of School Success*. Scarecrow Press: Landham, MD

As an example, Dr. Samples suggests labeling items in the home and making place mats that have pictures and words to look at while eating breakfast. These ideas are written for parents but appropriate for school personnel to read and share with families.. Some parents may wish to check this or similar books out of the school library. Other parents might prefer receiving a condensed list of ideas from the teacher. School staff can share ideas from web and magazine articles written for parents, as well.

Things to Do:

1. *Share the importance of family literacy with staff. Show the research regarding improved reading scores with the addition of family literacy programs.*
2. *Create a program such as a book club or backpack program for your school.*
3. *Keep accurate records of student reading comprehension for both pre– and post–family literacy program implementation.*

83. Night Owl Technology

It is hard to believe that there is anyone left in our country who does not have regular access to the Internet. I would argue there is no longer an average Internet access number or percentage in the United States. Many suburban communities have virtually all of their families connected, while other schools in urban or rural areas still report up to sixty percent of families without internet access. Perhaps the day will come when every American has affordable access to the Internet, but that day is not here quite yet.

Working with your community and business partners, open your school computer labs and library for family use during the evenings. Work with local businesses and educational grants to find the funding for monitors during these sessions. Promote family computer use at schools throughout the community, and encourage all families to use the service. Teachers can create assignments and family educational outreach ideas around computers and the Internet.

Things to Do:

1. *Work to find computer resources for families. Check with local business partners, the library, and similar entities that can help with the project.*
2. *Configure your school such that families can access computer labs in the evenings. Look for grants, or create a plan and present it to local businesses for funding.*
3. *Record the families who are utilizing the technology services. Ensure that all parents and families are using the services provided.*

84. Community Connections for Home Learning

When job and time constraints may prevent a family from walking through the front doors of a school to access a computer or obtain the novel for ninth grade literature, consider taking the novel and the computer to a location that is more convenient for the family. Local libraries and churches have hours and resources that extend beyond the traditional school day. Given the inherent desire of both organizations to promote community outreach and support education, libraries and churches are a great conduit for home learning.

Contact local churches and libraries and request one or more of the following:

1. A person on staff who would be trained in assisting families with online access to school web logs, grading programs that allow families to check attendance and grades (if applicable), material and resources on the local school and school district Web sites, and online resources that link to specific classes and school projects.
2. An area at the church or library where the school could provide a syllabus for each class, additional copies of novels, sample projects, etc.

Things to Do:

1. *Determine locations of prominent local churches and libraries where students in your community frequently visit.*
2. *Identify a staff member who can coordinate a site survey to determine if the off–site location has computer and internet access, staff available during non–school hours (evenings and weekends), and an atmosphere conducive to studying.*
3. *Provide the necessary training and materials to equip staff to assist families. When necessary, provide paper and toner for families and students to print school–appropriate materials (consider business partnerships to fund such materials.)*
4. *Publicize through a variety of media (church bulletin, school newsletter, flyer at athletic events, school Web site, local newspaper, etc.) the opportunity for families to access educational and online resources at the local library or church. When possible, provide*

hours of access and a specific point of contact so families can request assistance by name.

85. Dinner for Home Learning

With a gentle nudge from No Child Left Behind (NCLB), school leaders are increasingly focused on the academic achievement of specific subgroups of students and are developing interventions that target the needs of those students and their families. For example, consider the achievement of students with disabilities on high school graduation tests.

Over a period of years, the requirements of NCLB clashed with the educational and social realities inherent in many students with disabilities: Students did not understand the significance or the proficiency needed to pass the tests. Families were interested in helping their children prepare for the exams, but often did not have adequate knowledge of what content was included on the tests. Few formative assessments and valid practice exams were available for students or their families to accurately determine whether the student was on track to pass the high–stakes exam.

History has a way of repeating itself. In the absence of significant curricular, instructional, or assessment modifications, student test scores remain remarkably consistent within NCLB subgroups and content areas from year–to–year. Therefore, with regard to home learning, what can we do differently to prepare students and their families for success?

Things to Do:

(Example Specific to NCLB Subgroup—Students with Disabilities):
1. *Develop student profile to serve as indicator for success or areas of weakness.*
   a. *Pre–test all students with an assessment measure that links to the standardized test.*
   b. *Analyze grades in courses that correlate to domains on the standardized test. For example, performance in U.S. History is an indicator for success on the U.S. History domain of the graduation exam.*
   c. *Collect supplemental data that links to student achievement— attendance, discipline, etc.*
2. *Request (through payment or on volunteer basis) that case managers of students with special needs be available on a designated evening*

to meet with every student (and family) who will be taking the graduation exam.

    a.   Send an invitation letter from the principal.

    b.   Ensure that the case manager follows up with a phone call during the week of the event.

3.   Provide dinner and childcare for all families, students, and staff present at the event.

    a.   Dinner – consider donations from local businesses when funds are limited.

    b.   Childcare – utilize student clubs, organizations, or teams interested in community service hours.

4.   Have the case manager meet individually with each student and family to review their student profile (see #1 above) as an indicator of strengths and areas of concern relative to the graduation exam.

5.   Provide families with paper and online materials to promote home learning.

86. A New Twist on the Weekly Folder

Most parents and families are familiar with the elementary school ritual of the weekly folder. On a predetermined day, all elementary children (and some middle school students) bring home a folder of work completed in the previous five school days. Teachers use the folders to communicate with parents about a variety of issues. Families review the folder and, upon completion, sign and return the folder to the classroom teacher. There is a widely held belief that this type of communication supports the academic success of the students and keeps families apprised and abreast of classroom happenings. It does...sort of.

Consider for a moment the notion of parental efficacy, the empowerment of parents and families to have a hand in the education of their own children. Families reviewing completed work have little opportunity to become engaged with their children's learning and are likely to see the exercise as non–purposeful or worse yet, irrelevant. The experience quickly becomes a mundane process of checkmarks or signatures without a real focus on learning.

But what if the folder included samples of work for the following week at school? Would parents be more effective in helping their children prepare for the upcoming lessons? Folders filled with completed work may open the doors for families to "re–teach" skills not mastered, but folders filled with upcoming work provides an opportunity for families to "pre–teach," possibly giving the student just the boost to shine in the classroom the following week.

I have given this advice to thousands of educators across the country and have received numerous notes and e–mails with comments like, "What an easy solution to enhance the folder," and "Thanks for the great tip...it works." However, not everyone agrees with the idea of making the folder completely about the future. Many educators give strong and logical reasons for sharing completed student work with parents. Therefore, there is a compromise solution. Divide the folder in half. On the left hand side, include samples of work completed. On the right hand side, include information on upcoming lessons and learning. Next week, the left hand side of the folder will make a great deal more sense and have more meaning for families if they had a week to absorb the lessons and support their children.

Instead of asking parents and families to sign the form, consider a format that solicits more feedback. Ask what they thought about the completed work, or ask if they have any questions about the work to be completed. Better yet, include an activity that parents can do with their children, and give them a channel to report to you on their experiences.

This simple shift in the purpose of the weekly folder can exponentially improve home learning for all families.

Things to Do:

1. *Work with your grade level or team and discuss how the weekly folder can enhance home learning.*
2. *Begin to include examples of upcoming lessons and work to give parents and families an opportunity to know what is coming up.*
3. *Expand the family feedback form to elicit responses and questions from families to promote real dialog regarding learning.*

87. How Long Does the Homework Take?

I can remember those rare days when I successfully got my son to complete his homework. There were those occasions when the discussion about the importance of completing the homework lasted longer than the actual completion of the homework itself. Conversely, I recall long nights and heightened stress and frustration when homework assignments did not go well. Throughout all of those experiences, I remember thinking how much easier it would have been if I had some idea of how long the particular homework assignment should take.

Many schools have homework policies and share with families that they can expect a certain amount of nightly homework. These blanket policies, however, do not account for individual homework variances among teachers. There is a simple solution. Share with families how long the homework should take, and ask them to provide you feedback on the actual amount of time the student needed to complete the work.

If it was a thirty–minute assignment and the student spent three minutes, or three hours, this type of information goes a long way in helping teachers check for learning and understanding.

Things to Do:

1. *Create a mechanism using telephone, technology, or written word to share the length of homework assignments with parents and families.*
2. *Create a mechanism for all families to report back as to the length of time spent on homework.*
3. *Invite two–way communication in the support of home learning by encouraging responses from all parents and families.*

88. Help Families Be Tutors

Many times we overlook a fundamental need of all families—the need to be teachers for their children. In addition to giving parents ideas on content, create a "how to" guide for parents and families to become better tutors.

It is easy to overlook this issue. We make an assumption, as educators, that since we know how to help our children appropriately, that other families know how to do the same. Many families do not know teaching pedagogy and methodology. When teachers share this information with parents, the parents can extend *the classroom* teaching practices at home.

Help families understand the difference between "knowledge" questions and "application" questions. Help them understand good techniques for tutoring, most especially, how to guide their children toward an answer as opposed to asking a few times and then telling them. In cases where parents need to give the answer, instruct them to offer an additional problem so that the children can use the learning process and discover the answer on their own.

These sound like very simple and trivial suggestions. In fact, the beauty is the simplicity. It is quite simple for teachers to share aspects of their craft so that parents and families can become better teachers of their children.

Things to Do:

1. *Determine appropriate tutoring and teaching methodology that is transferable to families.*
2. *Provide easy instructions that are free of jargon. Tell them what information to present and how to tutor and reinforce the concept.*
3. *Ask parents and families for feedback to determine if your help was useful to them.*
4. *Take opportunities to celebrate parents and families who are improving their children's skills through better tutoring.*

89. Study Boards

Once again, I turn to Kim Bauerle, Family Engagement Specialist in Anaheim, California, for this excellent idea to support home learning. The concept of study boards is not only a great idea to support home learning, but is a wonderful activity for families and children to accomplish together, and is appropriate for all students, from elementary to high school.

Many families do not have a dedicated learning or homework area in their home, many times due to space restrictions. A homework board is a piece of cardboard and can be stored between the kitchen counter and refrigerator or other narrow space.

A study board usually begins with a three–paneled cardboard display board similar to the ones commonly used for science fair projects. Host an event at school, and give each family a study board, construction paper, glue, markers, etc., to design their own board. Invite families and students to use personal pictures to decorate the board. The board can have an assignment or homework section, a project section, a planning section, a calendar section, a things–to–do section, etc. The board promotes student organization and helps families and children focus on schoolwork.

Whenever homework time comes, families can pull out the board, set it up on the kitchen or dining room table, and have an instant home learning area. Homework assignments can be posted, and the calendar can be updated not only with assignments but with activities as well. The board encourages dialog between families and their children, and families can ask better questions about school assignments and activities.

Occasionally someone in our workshops will share a perception that the activity is very "elementary oriented" and not conducive to middle or high school students. Kim quickly reminds participants that she has led numerous workshops for hundreds of families in making these boards, and she works in a high school district. All of the boards are used in homes of secondary students! The idea is wonderful and universal.

Things to Do:

1. Collect the necessary materials — project board, paper, scissors, glue, etc.
2. Schedule a workshop for parents and families, or incorporate the activity into pre–determined events.
3. Guide families and their children through the process of creating the board.
4. Use your digital camera to take pictures of the final projects. Promote the success in the school or on the school Web site.

90. The Library as a Tutor

There is no question that many students need a great deal of support and encouragement to become academically successful. Many parents and families do not have the luxury of paying money for professional tutoring through various types of private learning institutions. The best way to support the need for tutoring is to expand community resources.

Collaborate with your local library system. Determine what role the library can play in tutoring children in need. The library can offer support, technology, software programs, space, and expertise to families in need of supporting their children academically.

Often your school librarian can make the initial contacts and find the appropriate inroads to public or community library systems. Many community libraries will be agreeable to loading school tutoring software programs to give parents and families access during non–school hours. (Check your software licensing agreement, so you do not break copyright or usage agreements.) Do not discount college libraries as a resource as well. In fact, local colleges are a wonderful place to find tutors for reasonable prices or college students who are interested in community service. Let all families know that there are wonderful tutors and resources available in the local libraries. Shoot some video of the tutoring "in action," and use it as a promotional tool on your school Web site. (Maybe the local library will post the video too!).

Things to Do:

1. *Approach your local/community library about expanding and supporting tutoring for families.*
2. *Determine what materials are available that can be shared with the local library. Be sure that materials match the standards and curriculum being taught.*
3. *Publicize the library tutoring, and celebrate the success!*
4. *Provide incentives for those families who use the library–based tutoring services.*

91. Family Didn't Attend? No Problem!

In time, you will cultivate a strong following of families. With any success you experience, there will still be those families who do not or cannot attend pre–arranged meetings or workshops. Get into the habit of having a backup plan to provide the information to absent families.

A very successful and practical means to share the contents of a workshop is to video or audio tape your program and make the tapes available to families who did not attend. A wonderful way to promote engagement and to build trusting relationships is to package the videotape with any handouts and a note similar to this:

> *Dear Mrs. Smith,*
>
> *I am sorry I missed you at yesterday's Math Counts workshop! I wanted to make sure you received all of the materials that we shared with families. Enclosed is a videotape of the meeting [or DVD, etc], the handouts, and other materials we shared with parents and families. If you have any questions about these materials, please do not hesitate to call me at XXX–XXXX, or if you prefer e-mail, teacher@school.com. In addition, I want to remind you of our next Math Counts workshop in two weeks. I will call you to remind you next week. Thanks for all you do!*
>
> *Sincerely,*
>
> *Teacher*

Make a home visit, and try to deliver the tape and documents personally. If that is impossible, leave the materials near the front door or with a neighbor. You might consider a neat looking package or something that identifies the package as "friendly," as opposed to a manila envelope, which can be interpreted as "bad news." We know from research that parents and families who are reluctant to attend meetings and workshops will watch the tape and review the materials.

Things to Do:

1. Work with your technology teacher or department to have your workshop videotaped.
2. Take attendance and create a list of those parents whom you very much wanted to be there but were absent.
3. Copy the appropriate number of tapes and materials.
4. Create small *"gift"* packages that look friendly and are not suggestive of bad news.
5. Make a home visit and deliver the materials. Make the personal face–to–face contact to continue to build a trusting relationship.

92. A Different Dialog for Engagement

There are times when helping families to engage in the academic lives of their children can simply be a matter of changing the dialog between families and children. Help families improve upon the standard question, "What did you do in school today?" Teachers can write a few questions about classroom topics and give families questions (and answers), so they can engage their children and reinforce learning at home.

All teachers can incorporate the following phrases into academic communication with families to foster more home support for classroom learning.

1. Tell me about…
2. Show me…
3. Teach me what you learned today…
4. Explain the difference…
5. How do you get …

These sentence and question prefixes help all create new dialog about school with their children. Sometimes parent work schedules are not complementary to having these types of discussions with their children. Remind families that they can ask their children to place work on the kitchen table. In addition, write questions with an expectation that the child will answer them in writing and leave them for the parent when he or she gets home from work. There are numerous creative ways to help families interact with their children. Always remember to close the communication loop by asking for feedback from families. Either invite them to let you know how the question techniques worked, or give them a call and ask. Better yet, drop by and see them at their home! While you are there, you can share other ideas and engage in positive conversation about school.

Things to Do:

1. *Create a standard template that promotes and helps parents and families to "ask better questions" of their children about class assignments, projects, curriculum, standards, etc.*

2. *Target families of children that need the extra support and improved engagement.*

3. *Communicate your desire to help them by telephone or personal visit.*

4. *Share and explain the "ask better questions" form. Get families to commit to trying it.*

5. *Create a structure for feedback from families. It could be a note back, a phone call, an e—mail, or the topic of conversation at the next meeting or home visit.*

93. Family Interactive Lesson Plans

Kim Bauerle first introduced this concept to me several years ago. It is a simple yet effective way to promote home learning for families. An interactive lesson design has as its core a simple question: How can the teacher extend the lesson into the home?

Interactive plans are not designed to be created every day. Periodically, teachers should take a lesson plan and make it interactive. The basic format of the plan is the same as a normal lesson plan (objective, content standard, lesson introduction, learning activity, closure, strategies, plan for assessment, summary evaluation). What is different about an interactive lesson is the consideration of how families can support the lesson at home.

Objective: The parent/family and child will be able to...
Standard: The parent/family and student understand...
Lesson/Student Learning: The child and parent/family will...
Summary Evaluation: The student will report the work done in collaboration with the parent/family...

Be sure to take into consideration cultural backgrounds and abilities. Also, when assigning an interactive lesson, give the assignment a week for completion to incorporate a weekend and account for different family structures and schedules.

Things to Do:

1. *Choose six to ten lessons per year that might be appropriate to transform into interactive lessons for families.*
2. *Follow the normal process of creating your plan, but keep at the forefront of your mind outcomes for students and their families.*
3. *Encourage and thank those families and students who use the interactive lesson!*

94. What Is a Standard?

No Child Left Behind.
Testing.
Standards.

These three terms have entered our daily lexicon. We desperately need our families to assist us at home in supporting the learning that is taking place in school so that our students will perform well on required tests. It can be a difficult task to share information about content standards, curricular strands, objectives, and outcomes with all families. When we do, we often assume that parents and families understand basic concepts of the learning that must take place.

It is difficult to explain the ever–changing topography of standards to parents and families so that they may assist and support their children with learning. Many teachers work hard to share content standards with families. But often, families do not understand why the specific learning is necessary or needed. Who made these standards? Where did they come from? A good idea to support home learning is literally to "back up" a step and share with parents and families not only what the content standard is, *but also what a standard itself is.*

Parent involvement expert Anne Henderson wrote a wonderful booklet a few years back titled, "Urgent Message for Parents."[9] She explains standards and why we have them in education. Follow these basic steps in communicating standards to families:

Explain to Families Exactly What a Standard Is: A standard says what something should be. It sets a goal. In education, standards say what children should know and be able to demonstrate through their learning. Most standards, but not all, are set by subject and/or grade level, or a combination of both.

Explain why Standards Matter: As students travel from school to school, whether it is in one district or across districts, without standards, their learning would not be congruent. They would learn different things in different places without regard to what curriculum might say is the learning outcome for a particular grade or subject.

---

9   The booklet is now out of print, but is available through ERIC documents. ED418480

Further, a discussion of low standards and high standards would be in order. Helping parents understand terms like *performance assessment*, *portfolios*, and *rubrics* would be helpful in promoting a thorough understanding of how and why we teach what we teach, and when we teach it.

Things to Do:

1. *Develop a process to relate standards information to the families of all of your students.*
2. *Publish the information in written and electronic format in multiple languages.*
3. *Use the standards information as a basis for making home visits.*

95. Saturday Academies

The concept of Saturday School is not new. Unfortunately, it often has a negative connotation as being part of a discipline program, as depicted in the movie *The Breakfast Club*. The type of Saturday Academy promoted here has an academic focus. During the summer, teachers can work together to identify areas of weakness in their student performance data. This data becomes the foundation of a "Saturday Academy Program."

The decision as to the length and duration of the Saturday Academy is one best made at your school. Having an isolated Academy on one Saturday morning, however, will not produce any visible or tangible benefit. The Academy should be a program or process that has multiple sessions and focuses on parents getting tips and information to support their children at home. While students benefit from the program, it should include and focus on families.

The requirement for multiple sessions is to give parents and families an avenue to report their success in implementing what they learned in the academy, and to seek further clarification or assistance. The Saturday Academy allows families to come together again to share experiences and learn from teachers and other families how best to support their children.

Things to Do:

1. *Identify strands and objectives that need to be emphasized during the coming school year based on student achievement data.*
2. *Create a series of Saturday Academies that provide families with the knowledge, tools, and strategies to support the home learning of their children in areas of assessed weakness.*
3. *Use the strategies for engaging the disengaged (personal invitation, refreshments, reminders, transportation, and childcare) to promote the attendance of families who can most benefit from the sessions.*
4. *Video tape or audio tape the session and provide it to those families who did not attend.*
5. *At the following seminar, provide an opportunity for families to discuss the ideas and strategies they implemented.*

96. Family Literacy Classes

We traditionally do a great deal of work in promoting reading in the home. Often, however, we forget to ask ourselves, "What if a parent cannot read or read well?"

According to the National Center for Family Literacy (NCFL), the following statistics should make a compelling case for schools to understand the need to promote family literacy:[10]

- Parental literacy is one of the single most important indicators of a child's success. The National Assessment of Education Progress (NAEP) has concluded that youngsters whose parents are functionally illiterate are twice as likely to be functionally illiterate themselves.
- By age four, children who live in poor families will have heard 32 *million* fewer words than children living in professional families will have heard.
- One in five, or 20 percent, of America's children five years old and under live in poverty.
- Some thirty million adults in the United States have extremely limited literacy skills. If one teacher could teach one hundred adults to read, we would need three hundred thousand adult education teachers to meet this need.
- The Hispanic population is the largest minority in the United States and has the highest school dropout rate. More than two in five Hispanics living in America age twenty–five and older have not graduated from high school

Things to Do:

1. *Learn all you can about the importance of family literacy by visiting the Web site for the National Center for Family Literacy (www. famlit.org).*
2. *Plan and execute processes for family literacy centered on those students who need reading support.*

---

10   http://www.famlit.org/site/c.gtJWJdMQIsE/b.1351223/k.6392/Family_Literacy__ You.htm.

97. Every Event as a Takeaway for Learning

Dr. Karen Mapp makes a wonderful analogy about education and Coke.

The Coca–Cola Company understands the importance of leveraging every opportunity for imprinting their brand on customers and potential customers. They never let an opportunity go by when they have potential customers to share their product and brand. Coke often has free taste tests and provides free soft drinks to millions of people in thousands of organizations. Customers take away the Coke message and brand.

Educators have multiple venues to host parents and families. Meetings, plays, concerts, musicals, workshops, back–to–school nights, and conferences are just a few examples. Often, we work hard to get parents to participate and then let the event go by without "promoting our brand," which in our case is giving parents a takeaway that promotes learning at home. Maybe it is a bookmark or a small multiplication table. Maybe it is a small book or calculator donated by a local merchant. Maybe it is a list of tips and practices parents can use to support specific learning or behavioral outcomes. Whatever the case, do not let that opportunity go by to give parents a takeaway to support home learning.

Things to Do:

1. *With your calendar in hand, note all of the events at your school to which parents will be invited.*
2. *Create an academic takeaway for each event.*
3. *The takeaway should contain information and help the parents support the learning of their children at home.*
4. *Work with business partners to leverage funds to provide small educational items such as calculators, books, or learning supplies.*
5. *Make every event a home learning event.*

98. "Lunch n' Learn" for Families on the Go

If you have not done so already, read the strategy entitled, "Outreach, Outreach, Outreach." (Increased Degree of Engagement, Strategy #61) This strategy is based on the philosophical foundation of outreach as a key to supporting home learning and the academic achievement of all students.

Many family members work long hours, and getting time off can be difficult. Parents who are hourly wage earners often have to give up a few hours' salary to participate in conferences or other school activities, whether they are during the day, at night, or on Saturday. Instead of bringing parents and families to your key workshops, bring the workshops to their work!

Contact the management at places of business where families work. Share your desire to help families become more engaged with their children's education. Ask if you can use a conference or break room too present a mini workshop during the employee's lunchtime. Call it the "Lunch n' Learn" session. This takes no time from the employees' work hours and benefits parents, school, employers, and especially children. Ask the business to publicize the "Lunch n' Learn" session.

Design a brief workshop for parents that focuses on one aspect of learning and provides them an activity that they can do with their children at home. While you have them there, have them fill out a small card and provide you with ideas for future "Lunch n' Learn" sessions. In addition, you may wish to ask the management of the business if they would recognize or perhaps provide some incentive for those employees who gave up an unencumbered lunch period to help their children. That kind of recognition will go a long way to encourage other parents and families to attend the next session.

Things to Do:

1. *Approach local businesses, offices, etc. about conducting "Lunch n' Learn" sessions for employees who have children at your school.*
2. *With the help of the business, publicize the dates to let these employees know of the upcoming seminar.*

3. *Assume you have no more than thirty minutes in which to teach a concept and provide an activity for families to use with their children at home.*
4. *Provide a takeaway activity for families.*
5. *Ask families to fill out an evaluation that gives you ideas of their needs for future "Lunch n' Learn" sessions.*
6. *Ask the management of the business to recognize those employees who participated in the "Lunch n' Learn" session.*

99. A Different Ed TV

With most families having access to hundreds of television channels and the Internet, it can be daunting to determine not only what is and is not appropriate for children's viewing, but what, if anything, is available that can support or enhance classroom learning. There is no question that a large number of television channels and Internet sites can be inappropriate for children. There are those, however, that are not only appropriate, but can enhance curriculum in the classroom.

The Discovery Channel, the History Channel, and the Learning Channel are three examples of networks that provide learning and thoughtful information that can support learning. Internet sites such as *math.com* and the *homeworkspot.com* not only offer guidance and assistance, but also provide sample problems and processes to reinforce learning. Check schedules and Web sites and let parents and families know that this support is available. It can even be incorporated into interactive lessons (see #93). Parents and families will be grateful and most will watch or participate in the learning, if you ask them.

Things to Do:

1. *Work with your school technical support staff and library to determine television channels and Web sites that are available to help families support learning at home.*
2. *Many television channels offer a monthly listing of programs. Check the listing for programs that support the particular curriculum or lesson you wish to introduce.*
3. *Create interactive lesson designs that involve the family either viewing a program together or working on a particular Internet site.*
4. *Give parents and families an opportunity to provide feedback to you on their experiences.*
5. *Celebrate successes!*

100. Vocabulary Lists at Home

I can barely remember my undergraduate years, but I do remember all of the creative ways in which I tried to study for a test. Often, the commencement of my studying was a bit late. Therefore, I always searched for the next best method of "cramming" information into my head for the swiftly approaching test. I do remember a friend suggesting that I write down on large sheets of paper the word or phrase that I needed to remember and then post those all over my dorm room. Through mental osmosis, I was supposed to absorb the information and would do well on my test.

I either cannot or do not wish to recall how I did on those tests for which I engaged in this process, but I did get out of undergraduate school and effectively used the same process at the graduate level. The idea of providing home vocabulary lists falls along the same continuum. Provide vocabulary words to families, and instruct them to make what amounts to large flash cards. Place them on the refrigerator, or over a dinner plate, on the kitchen cupboard, and over the coat hook. Use the same concept to learn rules of vocabulary, foreign languages, and math properties. Try it…it works!

Things to Do:

1. *Create a vocabulary list (or other informational sheets) and send to parents and families. Instruct them to make, or make for them, a series of small postings with the information on the posting. The sheet does not have to be bigger than a standard sized piece of paper and can be easily copied and distributed to families. This works particularly well when you are providing parent and family workshops on specific curricular issues as well.*

2. *Instruct parents and families to post these information sheets around the house, and encourage dialog about the information. Help families be creative and make the learning fun.*

3. *Give parents and families an opportunity to provide feedback and information as to their experience with the process.*

101. Create Content Study and Skills Guides

There is no better way to promote learning at home than to create documents for parents and families that not only help them understand learning, but help them support and encourage learning at home. The creation and use of study guides and study skills guides is a surefire way to promote home learning. The idea for these guides is also appropriate at any level, from kindergarten through high school.

Dr. Grant Rivera and the faculty of South Cobb High School worked to determine how best to help parents and families become involved and support students for the state graduation exam that is taken by every junior. The exam is a compilation of learning from grade nine and is the test that determines the school's ranking with regard to adequate yearly progress. After much thought, brainstorming, and deliberation, the content–specific "Family Guide to Preparing Your Student for the Graduation Test" was created in the core testing subjects.

Teachers in each of the subjects worked on creating an understandable and easily read guide for the families. They avoided the use of jargon while identifying and explaining key terms and concepts. Dr. Rivera made sure that both teachers and parents understood the concept and vision for the manuals. He was not concerned that families knew the material, but he wanted them to know and be able to determine if their children knew the material. This concept was the driving force behind the manuals.

CD–ROMs with the booklets in multiple languages were available, and numerous family workshops and events were held to help parents and families use the newly created materials. Hundreds of booklets, CD–ROMs, and other materials were distributed throughout the community. Evidence of success came when the school launched a series of Saturday Academies to help students prepare for the test. Approximately 150 students attended the academy with families eager to ensure their children's success.

Things to Do:

1. *Work in curricular teams to determine the types of content guides most beneficial for parents and families.*
2. *When developing the guides, avoid jargon and identify key concepts, vocabulary, and test areas.*

3. *Offer the guides in multiple ways—paper, CD–ROM, Web site downloadable, etc.*
4. *Host workshops and meetings to help parents and families use the guides to support their children at home.*

ACKNOWLEDGEMENTS

Special thanks to the following people for their contributions:

Linda Abram, Family Engagement Coordinator, North Penn School District, Lansdale, PA
Tess Blumenthal, Principal, Valley Elementary School, Jefferson, MD
Jane Gable, Carver Elementary School, Mt. Olive, NC
Anne Henderson, Washington, D.C.
Valerie Johnson, Woodley Hills Elementary School, Fairfax, VA
David LaRose, Superintendent, South Kitsap Schools, Port Orchard, WA
Karen Mapp, Graduate School of Education, Harvard University
Ryan Maxwell, Assistant Principal, Sunnyside High School, Sunnyside WA
Steve Myers, Superintendent, Toppenish School District, Toppenish, WA
John O'Meara, Principal, Yea High School, Yea, Victoria, Australia
Mike Smith, President, Differencemakers, Ltd.
Ed Wong, Principal, Ensign Intermediate School, Newport Beach, CA
The Boston Public Schools
The Canandaigua School District, NY
Hickman County Schools, TN

A special "thank you" goes to Kim Bauerle, family engagement coordinator for the Anaheim Union High School District. Kim has been a great friend and colleague for years and is an endless supply of ideas, enthusiasm, and support for families. You will see her name peppered throughout this book attached to wonderful and real ideas.

Writing a book can be a daunting task. Had it not been for Dr. Grant Rivera, Principal of South Cobb High School in Cobb County, Georgia, I suspect this book would never have been completed. He accepted my request for help and took responsibility for idea generation, organization, and some of the writing. We have worked on numerous ideas and projects together, providing each other encouragement when necessary. Even though his full time job as a high school principal keeps him busy, he always found time to work on this project and assist me in the development of concepts and materials. Dr. Rivera is a firm believer in the power of engaging all families and you will see many references to the wonderful ideas and strategies that are in place each day at South Cobb High School. He is good friend and great administrator.

I owe a great deal of gratitude to my partner in Family Friendly Schools, Sam Bartlett. His belief in the vision of family engagement was the catalyst for our organization. We could not be successful without our team. Much appreciation and thanks goes to all of the staff who works so hard to make our partnership with schools successful. All of these people had a hand in creating this book.

Most importantly, I need to thank my wife, Peggie. She keeps all of our family plates spinning in the air while I travel the country and descend to my office at home. Peggie's influence and ideas, taken from her school and our many "sundeck chats," are found throughout this book. No husband could ever ask for a more caring, supporting, and loving spouse. I truly am the luckiest man in the world.

I also want to thank the countless number of education professionals everywhere who have partnered with us, and are using the Family Friendly Schools process to engage all families. They follow the battle cry to keep reaching out to the disenfranchised, and continue engaging all. Keep doing what you are doing…we celebrate the difference you make!

ABOUT THE AUTHOR

 Educator, author, consultant, parent, and one of the leading practitioners in the field of family engagement, Dr. Steve Constantino's mission is engaging families in the educational lives of children as a conduit to improved student achievement.

From 1995 to 2003, Dr. Constantino served as principal of Stonewall Jackson High School in Manassas, Virginia. During his tenure, Stonewall Jackson High School was transformed from one of the lowest performing schools in the state of Virginia, to *Time* magazine's 2001 School of the Year. Stonewall was named number one among all Prince William County High Schools in the percentage of students entering college and among the top ten percent of schools worldwide offering the International Baccalaureate Program.

Dr. Constantino founded Family Friendly Schools in 1999, and began to spread the message of family engagement across the country and around the world. Today, Family Friendly Schools serves school districts in 42 states, with a team of certified engagement specialists who work with educators, school boards, schools and school districts, to not only raise awareness for family engagement but to help educators put into place successful family engagement practices that maximize the achievement of all students. For more information about how the Family Friendly Schools process can engage families and create success for all students in your school, e-mail us at info@familyfriendlyschools.com, visit us at www.familyfriendlyschools.com or call 1–800–890–7794.

Dr. Constantino has authored two previous books. *Making Your School Family Friendly* and *Engaging All Families*.

Dr. Constantino resides in the Atlanta, Georgia area with his wife Peggie, who is a high school principal. Their son Matthew is a graphic designer.

CPSIA information can be obtained
at www.ICGtesting.com
Printed in the USA
FSOW02n0417090215
5083FS